WINNING IN TRAFFIC COURT

I fight my traffic tickets in court, on my own
....and I usually WIN. ANYONE CAN

By

Bryan FitzGerald

Revised and Expanded
ANNIVERSARY EDITION

Century International Publishing Company, Houston, Texas

Published by:

Century International Publishing Company
Houston, Texas, U.S.A.

Printed in the United States of America

Library of Congress Catalog Card Number: XX-XXXXXX
ISBN 978-0-9679173-2-0
1. Education
2. Law
3. Self-Help
4. Study Aids
5. Transportation

TABLE OF CONTENTS

DEDICATION

For Patsy, my beloved wife and soul-mate, whose love, support, devotion and encouragement have sustained and enriched me in ways that I could not describe with mere words. We are two who became one more than half a century ago. I attribute anything that is good in me to the care and example she has showered upon me.

DISCLAIMER AND WARNING

DISCLAIMER
This publication is designed and intended to present anecdotal material, based upon the actual experiences of the author, and the author's opinions and beliefs solely for the information and entertainment of the reader. It is sold with the explicit understanding that neither the author nor the publisher intend to offer, or are engaged in rendering legal advice, which can only be offered by an attorney licensed to practice law.

WARNING
The herein information is based upon actual events and experiences in the life of the author, and is believed and thought to be accurate. Neither the author nor the publisher assumes or accepts any liability in connection with the use of this information by the reader or any other person. If legal advice or other expert assistance is required by the reader or any other person, the services of a competent professional person should be sought.

INTRODUCTION

I initially decided to write this book in 1995. After years of sorties into the traffic courts in several different states, fighting my traffic tickets and usually winning I came to believe I had a story to tell that would be inspirational and entertaining.

I am not a lawyer, so I could not set out to write a manual of legal advice. Moreover, I *did not want to write a legal manual*. Thus: this is not a legal manual. Please take note of the Disclaimer and Warning page. This book is a presentation of collected anecdotes, stories, opinions and beliefs. In it, you will read about the opinions I hold and the beliefs I have, concerning the traffic courts system of our land. You will read stories of my own exploits in various traffic courts around the nation; what offenses I was charged with and how I took my cases to court and usually won.

At the root of the collected stories and anecdotes about my traffic court cases, you will find, spelled out in various ways, my strong commitment to use the system to secure victory. I passionately believe the system to be an unfair, archaic, corrupt and incompetent process that robs individuals and the nation's economy of tens of billions of precious dollars (yes, you read that correctly . . . read on). The process, in my humble opinion, does nothing to create better drivers and produces nothing of any value whatsoever to the overall society. It is a system that simply enlarges and perpetuates a counterproductive, parasitic and corrupt bureaucracy.

Sadly, not nearly enough people in this great nation exercise their rights. Too few people go to court to fight their traffic tickets.

Many, perhaps most, people are afraid to go to court. They are intimidated by the prospect. They fear the system, which is what the perpetrators of "the system" want them to do. As a result, we continue to lose more and more rights as the years go by. I am here to tell anyone who cares to listen that the emperor has no clothes. The system has no claws. The system has more to fear from those who exercise their rights than you might imagine.

It is my sincere wish that this book will serve as an inspiration to others; give them the courage to fight for their rights, and use the system to secure victory for themselves.

. . . TO THIS "REVISED AND EXPANDED ANNIVERSARY EDITION"

I planned to release the "Tenth Anniversary Revised Edition" in 2010. The events of the first decade of the 2000's that have so devastated our National Economy, our Spirits and . . . yes, I will include our Collective Will and our Moral Strength, made it impossible for me to meet that goal. Like most writers, I must do more than write to put food on the table and pay the bills.

The *first* week of 2009 marked the *last* week of my regular, full time employment that pays . . . or, rather *paid* the bills. Suffice it to say that the past few years have been less than luxurious . . . but very educational. So here we are about to release the "Revised, Illustrated and Expanded Anniversary Edition" of Winning In Traffic Court . . . on the Twelve Year Anniversary of the Original.

What you will find in this Edition is more . . . All of the original content expanded on to bring more clarity to the anecdotes and provide more insights into the tools I have used over the years as well as some of the newer available tools that are quite helpful. The Traffic Court system today is, in my own humble opinion, far worse, far more corrupt that it was when the Special Inaugural Edition of this book was released in 2000.

Now, more than ever, we need to stand up and defend ourselves and our families from the heavy hand of corruption that controls the operation of our nation's so-called traffic courts.

Oh, I know. There are many who say I am a fool on a fool's errand. "Just pay the damn ticket and get on with your life", I've been told more than once. My response is that the traffic court system amounts to nothing more than an organized system of stealing money from hard-working, decent people. In my view, stealing that goes unpunished tends to perpetually grow . . . and perpetual growth is the philosophy of *Cancer*. In the end it destroys you.

Want to put an end to the corruption and theft of your hard-earned money? Then consider these important details:
Let's say, for the sake of illustration, that of our 350 million people, 200 million traffic tickets are issued annually (probably a ridiculous under-estimate), with an average fine of $150.00 (including the tacked on penalties and fees – you see greed never stops growing, especially if is left unchallenged).

Those tickets (if all were paid) would generate . . . the incredible sum of $30,000,000,000.00. That's billion, with a B! Think about it, $30 Billion taken out of American's pockets . . . and out of the General Economy!

Now let's take it a step further . . . suppose all 200 million who received those tickets demanded their Constitutional right to a trial in court . . . perhaps even a *JURY TRIAL*. Are you paying attention?

My challenge to you is this: it is long past time to "man-up" and not be a sheep, led to the slaughter. You have the option to fight this corrupt system from within the system and keep your hard-earned dollars for yourself and your families. Use those dollars to create something worthwhile and good . . . not to perpetuate corruption of the American freedom that was passed on to you by others at great human cost.

You Can Do It! You Should Do It! You Must Do It!
While you still can.

DRIVE FRIENDLY!

FOREWORD

... HOW IT ALL BEGAN ...

For more than forty years, I have insisted on having my day in court on almost all of the traffic tickets I received over those many years. It all began when I was pulled over one day by a police officer who said he clocked me with his radar at 46 miles per hour in what was a 35 mile per hour zone. I was absolutely certain I was not driving that fast.

The officer wrote the ticket, handed it to me for my signature and then handed me my copy. As I looked over the ticket, I saw the officer pull over another driver and start writing her a ticket. He had not returned to his cruiser/radar unit, which was parked on a side street just off the corner of the boulevard with the wide center esplanade dividing it along which I and the other driver had been driving.

It was too late to go to the meeting I had been driving to, so I decided to return to my office. I pulled away from the curb, drove to the next intersection (the street where the officer's cruiser was parked) and made a U-turn. As I completed my turn, I saw the officer pull over yet another motorist. Again without having returned to his radar unit first. That was two tickets I saw him write without ever clocking the driver with his alleged radar gun, as I felt certain had been the case with me. I pulled over and parked. I watched the officer issue six more tickets without ever returning to his car. As I sat in my car watching the spectacle, I also focused on another important factor. There was a forty-foot long moving van parked on the boulevard, about twenty feet behind the point where I had parked, when the officer flagged me down. I was passing the van when I saw the officer waving me over to the curb.

Later, I measured distances and sketched out the scene where the officer had indicated on my ticket that he had clocked me. He would have had to aim his radar gun diagonally through that forty-foot long van to clock me where he said he had.

I went to court, questioned the officer and raised all of the points I mentioned above. I drew a sketch on the blackboard and got the officer's agreement as to the positioning of his and my vehicles and the placement of the parked van. Next, I drew a line directly from the officer's parked cruiser (where the radar was) diagonally through the entire length of the van. I told the officer it was my understanding that a radar unit could not clock a vehicle through a solid object and asked him to explain to the court how he could have done so. He scratched his head and said, "Hmmm?" I told the judge I had no further questions, fully believing I had won my case.

The judge complimented me on my presentation but allowed that he believed the officer was certainly competent and that there was, no doubt, some missing element in the "puzzle". He said he believed the officer would have had no reason to cite me if I had not committed the violation. He declared me guilty.

The judge very nearly held me in contempt when I told him what I thought of his decision. I resolved at that moment that never again would I be railroaded like that. I never have been.

CHAPTER ONE

Traffic Tickets. Who Gets Them, And Why?

Two groups, or classes, of people get traffic tickets: willful violators and erroneous violators. The willful violators are cited for something they did intentionally that violates a traffic law or laws. Erroneous violators are cited for a breach of a traffic law or laws that was un-intentional. Simple.

Yet, neither the law nor the court system makes any distinction between willful and erroneous violators. The finding of guilt or innocence for a violation of any traffic law is the same, whether the violation was intentional or not. If the violation is proved, the finding is guilty.

Those who have ever gone to court and pleaded "guilty with an explanation" have foolishly wasted their time. Furthermore, those people have also wasted the court's time. But, there's an upside, when you consider that it cost the system part of the money to extract the dollars that a guilty plea would have provided with no strings attached.

The issue is quite simple. If I am cited for a traffic law violation and I belong to what I believe is the larger of the two groups of people who get traffic tickets, the erroneous violators, I have simply been cited for making a mistake. If I plead guilty, or am found guilty at trial, I will then be punished for making an error, a mistake.

All across America, in courts everywhere, every business day, people are punished for making a simple mistake, an error in judgment, or a careless lapse in attention.   What is most significant, though, is that the un-intentional violation of a traffic law; the error in judgment; the careless lapse, the mistake itself, is often *not* the *why* of who gets traffic tickets.   Unfortunately, traffic tickets are a big business in America, a very big business. Too often, the *why* of who gets traffic tickets boils down to a police officer writing his *assigned quota* of tickets to generate the coveted revenue those tickets bring into cities, towns and municipalities.

These government entities often grow very fond of the dollars traffic tickets bring into the kitty. Greed has long since set in. I believe the *why* of who gets traffic tickets frequently is not the fact that a traffic law was violated, but that the jurisdiction wants the money. That is not intended to be a cynical statement. I honestly believe, after studying the issue for more than forty years, that the statement above is a true and accurate reflection of the reality of the situation.

Mistakes and Errors - Yours and Theirs.

Just as surely as I can make an error or mistake that results in a traffic ticket, so can the officer who cites me. The prosecutor who tries my case in court, or the judge who presides over the trial, can make an error that will result in victory for me in court. The whole court system is concerned with mistakes; errors. Later chapters will reveal both the significance and the potential negative or positive impact of mistakes on the process.

Anyone who has ever received a traffic ticket fell into one of the two groups, willful or erroneous violators.

I was a member of the willful violators' category if I intentionally violated the law. For example: I am driving home from my second shift job one Thursday night at twenty minutes until one in the morning. The traffic light two blocks from home turns red as I approach it. It's a two minute light. I have personally timed it. I have driven fifteen miles from my place of work and have seen only one other car on the road, about ten miles back. There are vacant fields on all four corners of the intersection and I can see a quarter mile in all directions. There is no approaching traffic. I decide I am not going to stop for a two minute red light to accommodate a flow of cross traffic that won't be there until the morning rush hour, about five hours hence. I want to go to bed. I'm tired. Just under two blocks further on, as I am preparing to turn left into my driveway, the glare of the solid red light and flashing blue lights from the police car reflects into my eyes from the rear view mirror. I hand over my license, the officer walks back to his cruiser, runs me through the computer as he writes out the citation and returns moments later. He invites me to "drive more carefully and have a good night", then hands me my "ticket" to traffic court.

No one has yet come up with the statistics on how many of the traffic citations issued annually are handed to willful violators. Usually, only the violator knows for certain if she or he intentionally violated the law.

I belong to the erroneous group if the action for which I am cited was not intentional. For example: I am driving along the Pacific Coast Highway on a beautiful spring morning. The traffic is very light, with several hundred yards separating the cars on the highway; the sun is glistening on the blue water of the Pacific Ocean. My favorite music is playing on the stereo as I reflect on the activities I have planned for the evening. It's a great day that couldn't be much better. That is, until I am disturbed by the noise of the highway patrolman's siren.

The patrolman greets me politely with a tip of his hand to his cap. "Good morning, sir. Do you know how fast you were driving?" he asks. I reply something like: "Well I'm not sure exactly how fast I was going. But I don't believe I was speeding. Was I?" The patrolman gives me the bad news that he observed I was driving seventy two miles an hour, which is seventeen miles an hour over the posted maximum speed. He appears almost embarrassed for me, for such a lack of awareness on my part. What a nice guy!

In a matter of moments, the great day I had been enjoying has disintegrated into a bleak, depressing one, as I read over the citation the patrolman has presented to me. When he pulls out onto the highway again and moves past me in search of yet another highway marauder, I am reading the part of the citation that informs me that I may appear in court one month hence, Promptly, at 8:00 A.M. . . . in Middle Podunk, a quaint hamlet ninety miles from my home.

Willful violators and erroneous violators . . . different; yet the same. The simple fact is, the law makes no distinction between the two. I believe the overwhelming majority of traffic citations are issued to people in the erroneous violator category. In many cases, perhaps most, the person has actually violated the section of the law for which the citation was issued. Does that mean the violator should plead guilty and pay her fine? Hardly! Nothing could be further from the truth, in my opinion.

To begin with, if I plead guilty, I will pay a lot more than the fine. I will also pay taxes and assessment fees. Most importantly, I will pay a higher premium on my auto insurance at my next renewal date, and for the succeeding three years! Think about that. The premium increase could be as much as fifteen percent. Thus, if I pay $500.00 semi-annually for my insurance, the premium could increase by $150.00 per year for the next three years. That's $450.00 in addition to the fine, penalty assessment and tax on the ticket conviction, which for a typical interstate highway speeding conviction may be as much as $120.00 or more.

Do you believe I should pay $570.00 over the next three years, simply because I inadvertently let my speed get up to seventy two miles an hour on a highway that was designed to handle traffic at speeds even greater than that? I certainly do not.

We have an adversary system in our courts. I am issued a citation for making an error which, allegedly resulted in my violating a traffic law. Unless I like the idea of paying $570.00 over the next three years for my indiscretion if, in fact, the charge is honest and accurate, I am going to have to exercise my right to go to trial and try to win the adversarial legal contest. That is *not* as daunting or difficult a task as many people believe.

The idea, when I go to trial in traffic court, is to do all I can to uncover and reveal that the officer who cited me also made an error that day, in the process of citing me. Failing that, I must make every effort to put the officer and/or the prosecutor and/or the judge in a position, during the course of the trial, to make an error that will enable me to win and cause them to lose the contest.

Police officers, prosecutors and judges are just human beings, like the rest of us, Mere Mortals. As a group, they are no more and no less intelligent than any other average group of people. They make mistakes as often as all the rest of us do.

As soon as I have determined I am about to be ticketed, I must begin my campaign to win my case in traffic court. In most cases, I would try to discuss the situation with the officer and try to get only a warning, without admitting that I had, in fact, committed any violation.

You may think my next observation is facetious. It is not intended to be. Nor, is it intended to be insulting to women. I love women; some of my best friends are women . . . in fact my number one best friend, my beautiful wife, is a woman. But I have informally

17

researched the phenomenon I am about to address, asking numerous police officers I know personally about their own experiences in such situations.

I am not an attractive or pretty woman . . . or even an average looking or not so attractive woman. I will tell you, though, that if I were, I would soak my hanky with the gusher of crocodile tears I would produce for the officer who pulled me over and intended to write a citation, even going to the length of crying hysterically and pleading for another chance . . . oh, how routinely I would use the tactic if I were a member of the fairer sex! My little research project, described above, produced staggering evidence to show that such a tactic is so powerful, it works overwhelmingly in almost all cases.

I have queried about twenty cops; friends and family members of mine, over many years. With the exception of only a few of them . . . four to be precise, they all told pretty much the same story . . . "I just can't stand to make a lady cry. It makes me feel like a real stinker. I can't get back to my cruiser fast enough."

As for the four "Stinkers", ladies, I can say only that the long odds in favor, make it an easy tactic worth a shot in my estimation. Oh, but I probably wouldn't try it on a female officer.
I'm just sayin' . . .

In my experience, it would be a rare exception if I received only a warning from the officer and was allowed to go on my way.

When the officer makes it clear that he or she is going to cite me, I take whatever immediate action I can to begin my campaign to win the case. If I am a long way from home, for example, in the far reaches of the county where I live, and the vehicle code in my state contains a provision that allows me to *instruct* the officer that I want the citation he is about to issue to be answerable at the central court of the county seat (which might be in the city where I live) seventy miles north (as was and may still be the case in the State of California), I will *immediately* give that instruction to the officer. I will instruct him that under article such and such, section so and so, of the vehicle code, I want the citation to be answerable at the central court of the county seat.

There are *important* reasons why I would take such action. First. If the officer refuses to make the citation answerable at the county seat, as the law provides, he will just about ensure my victory, if not in trial, then on appeal. The second reason is that by having the case tried in the Central Court at the County Seat, even if it is not the City where I live, it means that the officer has to travel outside his comfort zone to a far off court where he is as much a stranger as I am and his regular group of prosecutorial cronies are nowhere to be found in that strange courthouse.

If the citation requires me to appear at a place other than the central court of the county seat, I will immediately inform the officer that he has denied me my rights under the vehicle code, which is not optional. Then, when I appear at the court listed on the citation, as soon as my case is called, I will immediately submit my motion to the court (judge) for dismissal. That's when the fun begins.

To illustrate the *importance* of the action I take as soon as I know the officer is going to write me up, I will relate the details of one of my own cases. I will relate part of the story here. Other parts of the story will unfold in later chapters. I will call this the "San Diego Freeway Caper".

Driving south along the I 405 Freeway, on a business trip to San Diego, I was stopped by a California Highway Patrol officer in San Clemente, at the southernmost end of Orange County. The officer stopped me, he said, for speeding, at approximately 1:30 in the afternoon. At this point, I will not go into the details of the traffic stop itself and the circumstances surrounding it. Those are parts of the story I will reveal to you in later chapters. What I wish to relate to you here is what actions I took as soon as I was sure the officer was going to cite me.

When, after our initial dialogue, it was clear to me that the officer intended to write me a ticket, I asked him: "are you going to write me a citation?' He stated he was going to cite me for speeding, and I immediately said,"If you are going to cite me then, under section 40502 of the Vehicle Code, I want you to indicate on the citation that it is answerable at the central court of the county seat, in Santa Ana." The officer looked me in the eye and, with a little snicker, said "I can't do that". I returned his stare and said, "Yes you can do that. In fact, under section 40502, you have no other option. You must indicate the county seat as the place where this citation is answerable."

. . . . It's a funny thing about police officers, sometimes. They do not like to be told they must do something, especially by the person over whom they are exercising their *authority*, even when they know that they must. They tend to forget at those times that they are "public servants", who work for *us* . . . you know, the *Taxpayers* who pay their salaries. They also forget the laws apply to *everyone*.

I am certain this officer was intelligent enough to know that what I was demanding, I was entitled to, under the law. But, like many police officers, this fellow decided he was not going to be told what to do by a mere civilian. He wrote the ticket and made it answerable at the South County Court, in Mission Viejo. Mission Viejo is a long way from where I lived in Anaheim Hills.

He handed me the citation to sign my promise to appear and I said, "You have denied me my rights under the law and I assure you I will seek my remedies in court." The officer seemed to be struggling within himself to maintain his composure. "You do that", he said, and handed me my copy of the ticket.

Later on, I will relate more of the story of the San Diego Freeway Caper. You will see how the whole story played out, step by step, ending with a *very satisfying* victory for me in court. Actually, there were several victories along the way.

CHAPTER TWO

Why fight A Ticket In Court?

Not fighting the system, but using it.

In most cases, there is only one logical choice to make when I receive a traffic citation. *Go to court and fight it.* Does the decision to fight the ticket mean I am going to fight the system? Certainly not. On the contrary, choosing to fight my ticket in court is *using the system as it was intended to be used*.

I believe, in fact, that I have a duty to fight my ticket in court. Consider the fact that we Americans continue to lose precious rights that should be, and in fact once were, ours. For example: in certain states, the right to have a trial by a jury of my peers no longer exists for traffic violations, or certain other cases designated as *infractions cases*. The purported rationale for the loss of the precious right to a jury trial is that an infraction case supposedly does not put my liberty or my property in jeopardy.

Ask yourself a simple question. If I am found guilty and assessed a fine of $50.00, which when all of the taxes - yes taxes - and various other penalty assessments which are tacked onto the fine are added, will end up somewhere in the neighborhood of $100.00, is that $100.00 my property or not?

Furthermore, if I do not pay the fine and assessments, will I then go to jail? And thus, wouldn't being in jail severely impact my liberty?

You guessed it. Bad news!

But there is worse news to follow. In certain states, California for one, in an "infraction" case, such as a traffic case, the judge may, and frequently does, also act in the capacity of *prosecutor* in my case, actually acting against me, as my *adversary*. In other words, the prosecutor in my case - my *adversary* - whose job it is to press the case against me and seek a guilty verdict; he who presses this case and presents it to the court (*the judge*?) against me - may also **be the judge**? How much faith do you have in the justice that is likely to emerge from that skewed scenario? You will read more about this unholy alliance later.

The real problem is that too many people in America do not use the system. As a consequence the bureaucrats, who are not your friends by the way, have concluded that nobody is watching them; that they can do as they please. They are stealing our rights from us and getting away with it because we are letting them do it. There are serious corruptions in the judicial system and the system is beginning to crumble. Think! Consider what the loss of rights means to us, as American citizens. Then, do something positive about it. The loss of small rights, if unchallenged and unchecked, leads to the loss of ever greater rights in the future.

If a small rock strikes my car's windshield as I am driving along the highway and one of those small "star" cracks appears, I have options. I can repair the star crack, inexpensively, and prevent the loss of my entire windshield. Or, I can ignore the star crack and it will grow over time. At some point I will see a linear crack grow out of the star crack to a length of several inches. The several inch long linear crack may remain that way for days, weeks or months. At some undetermined point in the future, though, the crack will spread further. Ultimately, the windshield will have to be replaced. It will be destroyed. Lost. Gone.

Replacing or Recovering Rights, once they are lost to us is not analogous to replacing a windshield that we lost because we chose not to save and preserve it for a few dollars. Sure, it will cost a few hundred dollars to replace the windshield, instead of the few dollars it would have cost to preserve it. But the end game with the windshield is that you may be out a few hundred bucks, but you have your windshield again.

When we lose Rights . . . and we are discussing Rights here that were not purchased *by us* . . . they were purchased *for us* and at great human cost, **not a paltry handful of dollars**. I consider it a great shame and a disgrace when I observe so many of our numbers who have so little respect for the great gifts of Rights that were won for us and handed to us that they lack the courage and commitment to preserve those precious Rights.

If more of us do not exercise our option to use the system and protect out rights, ultimately, we will lose the system and have no rights. Buying a new windshield that I could have saved with a small investment would be expensive. Where would I go to buy a new Bill of Rights; and what would be the cost?

We may, one day, have to find the answer to that question and to suffer the cost.

CHAPTER THREE

Reading The Citation.

Searching for the easy win.

The first thing I do when I receive a traffic citation is *carefully* read the citation. I am looking for mistakes. Any error on the ticket is a potential for dismissal of the charge and victory for me. If the officer writes the wrong date on the ticket, makes a mistake on my driver's license number, my address or any other detail, I have grounds to move for dismissal.

It is important for me to keep focused on the issue of error. It was error that got me the ticket and it will probably be error that helps me win my case.

It is appropriate here to offer a few words of caution about errors on the citation.

On one occasion, I was returning home from my Thursday night choir practice at about 2:15 on a Friday morning. About two blocks from my driveway, I roused the officer from his peaceful slumber as he was "cooping" next to one of those mini warehouse facilities. There wasn't another car or pedestrian within five miles of me. It was late. As was our usual custom, several of us members of the Men's Choir of our parish church reconvened, after practice to a neighborhood beer garden to have a few beers and enjoy the pleasure of each other's company. The place was a family friendly, old time place, where everyone knew each other. The after practice gathering had become a tradition. Of the forty five men in the choir, probably twenty of them, on an average Thursday night, would gather at this beer garden after practice each week. It was a fine tradition.

We had some great discussions. We all enjoyed the company of our friends. We pitched washers, pitched horseshoes, talked politics and discussed a wide range of issues that were important to all of us. We were a very diverse group; everything from mechanics, to engineers, to accountants, to Ph.D. chemists. We were all like brothers and really enjoyed our Thursday sessions after choir practice.

The officer who stopped me that early Friday morning, was a guy who was very interested in a young lady who worked as a checker at the local supermarket. I knew the young lady from my many trips to the store, and we had developed a casual friendship. The first thing I did when the officer gave me the ticket that early Friday morning was read over the ticket. I had not gone very far before I started laughing. The officer had put the wrong date on the ticket. I was really tickled. This will be a blast, I thought. I was looking forward to going to court and winning this one on such a basic error by the officer.

Later that morning, after I had slept, I went to the supermarket for a few breakfast items. The officer's would be girl friend was working the register when I checked out. I told her I had gotten a ticket from her would be boyfriend earlier that morning and I laughed as I told her that I would enjoy the day when I went to court and won, because he had made the foolish error of putting the wrong date on the citation.

Well it seems to me I seriously misjudged the situation. I really did not think the officer had any real chance with this young lady. That notion was based on her comments from time to time, which had led me to believe she did not particularly care much for him.

Imagine my surprise when, about a week later, I received in the mail a revised citation, correcting the issue date. My initial reaction was that there was no way he could do that. The ticket was written; the date was wrong, and it was basically an irreversible error. I found out otherwise. Though I ultimately won the case by other means, the court *did* rule that the ticket could be amended *before the trial date* as long as I received a copy of the amended ticket before the trial date.

The lesson here is that I should have done my homework, studied the ticket for errors and developed a plan to exploit the error for the purpose of winning the case. I did those things. But I *should have kept my mouth shut* about my discovery of the mistake. I am quite certain the girl friend, or would be girl friend, of the officer in this case tipped him off to my discovery of his error. It could have cost me the case.

That experience taught me I need to study the ticket and, if I find an error, keep it to myself until the trial. Then, clobber the officer with his error and win the case.

CHAPTER FOUR

Documenting My Case.

Write it down - now...or lose it.

One of the most valuable lessons I have learned about fighting my tickets in court, I learned from my main adversaries, the officers who have cited me over the years. If you were to go to traffic court and just sit there to observe the proceedings, there is at least one thing you would see repeated over and over again. Every time an officer took the stand to testify, you would see the officer take out his notebook and refer to it throughout his testimony. In many, perhaps most cases, he would read verbatim from his notes and add nothing else unless he was asked or directed to.

The important point here is that the officer knows when he issues the citation to me that he may not even remember me after the period of time that would elapse before he would have to appear in court against me. Consider the fact that the officer may write dozens of tickets per week and it could be literally months before he would see me in court. Putting myself in his place, I have to ask the question: How much would I trust my memory to recall the details of a simple traffic citation, an event repeated over and over again, day in day out, week after week, month after month? Chances are, without written notes, I would remember little, if anything, about a traffic stop I'd made months ago. Officers are trained to write a summary of the details of the traffic stop. Some officers are quite good at it. Others do not do as well. I have an advantage over the best of them for several reasons.

First. Few people exercise their right to confront the officer in court and challenge him. Because the officers know the chances of ever having to see me in court are so remote, the summary in the officer's notebook will primarily describe what he stopped me for and any statements I made, either in response to his questions, such as: "Do you know how fast you were driving?", or that I made spontaneously of my own volition, like: "Gee, officer, I thought you guys only gave tickets for driving more than ten miles over the speed limit."

If I gave smart answers to his questions and did not make any goofy statements, his notes will be brief and not very helpful to him when he is faced with my well planned, serious challenge.

Second. By training myself to be smart whenever I have the misfortune of being stopped for a traffic offense; real or not, I make more observations than the officer will put into his notes, even though he is a professional.

I have seen many people waste their time going to traffic court to fight a ticket. The reason they wasted their time was that they went to court unprepared and the officer had his little notebook with the written comments he recorded right after he handed them the citation.

So, what's the lesson here?

I write it down! *I don't wait.* As soon as the officer pulls away, or if he lingers and I have to pull away first, I find a place to pull over off the road, and get out my own report form and pen or pencil. I write down every detail I can. While the officer is running me through the computer and writing the ticket, I look all around me, making mental notes of everything I see: the weather and road conditions, the amount of traffic, the lane I was driving in when I first saw the officer, as well as the lane he was driving in, or where he was parked.

I quickly reconstruct, in my mind, the positions and descriptions of the other vehicles that were around me and any other details I can identify. If I was stopped on a city street, I make notes of the nature of the street; business or residential; whether there were driveways along the street or entrances to commercial facilities; whether there were pedestrians in the area. I especially note any obstructions, such as overhanging trees or shrubs or objects or vehicles in the roadway which may have required me to accelerate and make a fast lane change to avoid a collision, or any other pertinent details.

In short, I write down everything I can, about the time, place, conditions and circumstances that could have any bearing on my case; in my favor *or against me*. My notes will be better than the officer's notes because I am more motivated than he is. *I will be better prepared in court than he is; not because I am smarter than him (though I may be), but because I am more motivated.* If he loses the case, it doesn't cost him any money. In fact, he is being paid for his court appearance - win or lose. If I lose, it will cost me hard earned dollars that rightly belong to my family. *This is not a game with me.* I have often had fun in traffic court, but I take the process seriously. I am not a wealthy person. I go to court to do all I can to keep my money for my family. *I never lose sight of that.* If I have some fun, occasionally, in the process of winning my case, it's like a little bonus. Of course just winning the case is its own reward.

At the end of this chapter I have included a report form that you can reproduce and use as is, or modify to suit your own preferences. Keep a few copies of the "TRAFFIC CITATION DETAIL REPORT" form in your glove box. Then you can start filling it out while the officer is running you through the computer. Yuou can finish the report after he hands you your ticket to the big event and goes on his way. Complete the report as soon as you can and add anything else of significance to the report. After you get home you can take a little time to review what you have written in the report and make any changes or additions you may want to include. Study the report from time to time prior to your trial date. Also, in the week or so before your trial date, you should outline and polish off your script for your own testimony and your questions for cross examination of the officer in trial.

It is also *important* to note that I *never* show disrespect for my adversaries. I treat them with the respect I expect to receive from them. I also respect "the system". No matter how corrupt I believe the system has become, it is still the law of the land and *the system within which I must conduct myself* in order to achieve my objective of winning my case. If I were to show disrespect for the system or any of the individuals who represent the system, I would lessen my chances of winning. This is not a hypocritical attitude. I do, sometimes, find ways to express my disappointment with the system and expose the ways officers sometimes cheat to make their jobs easier.

TRAFFIC CITATION DETAIL REPORT

JURISDICTION/ENFORCEMENT AGENCY
OFFICER NAME
EXACT LOCATION DETAILS
CHARGED VIOLATION
WEATHER/ROAD/TRAFFIC CONDITIONS
OTHER COMMENTS
CITATION DATE/TIME

CITATION LOCATION SKETCH:

GENERAL OBSERVATIONS:

ADDITIONAL COMMENTS:

(Note: Some additional suggested questions)
1. Did you admit to the charge?
2. Was your discussion confrontational?
3. Collision involved?
4. Witnesses/Names?
5. Unusual behavior by officer?
6. Anyone injured/how many/who's fault?
7. Radar stop/officer show radar gun?
8. Other unusual conditions?
9. Other significant details?
10. Initial placement your/officer's vehicles?

CHAPTER FIVE

Witnesses.

A margin for victory.

If a picture, as the old saying goes, is worth a thousand words, then a witness is probably worth a couple of thousand words. That is . . . ***if the witness is credible.***

Appearing in court, on my own behalf, to fight a traffic ticket is not something that strikes fear into my heart. I am always confident that I can win my case. The basis for my confidence is the fact that I do my homework. I prepare myself and my case well in advance of the court date; I begin preparation of my defense while the officer is going through the process of preparing the citation against me.

It goes without saying that one of the first things I am going to do is to determine if there is any person or persons who may have witnessed the events that led to my being cited by the officer.

As I go through the process of preparing my notes after receiving a citation, one of the things I try to find is a friendly witness; a live, credible person who witnessed the events and feels, as I do, that I was not guilty of the infraction for which I have been cited.

It is interesting to me that the people who linger at a location where an officer is citing someone for a traffic violation seem to fit into two groups. There are those who feel that anyone who is stopped by an officer is guilty of whatever the officer thinks he or she is guilty of. Then there are those who believe the officer is either wrong or being unfair; that the driver does not deserve the citation for one reason or another.

If there is a friendly witness nearby, I can usually spot the person. He or she will usually make eye contact with me and give me some sign, such as a shake of the head, to let me know that he or she is "on my side". If I see such a sign from someone nearby, I will try to engage the person in conversation while the officer is back in his cruiser running me through the computer, or I will wait until the officer has left.

After a few minutes of friendly conversation with the person, if I believe I have a good prospective witness, I will ask if the person would consider coming to court as a witness for me. I have never been able to determine what moves people to agree to appear as a witness. It would seem that the degree of inconvenience would be a major factor. Yet, there are people who would be substantially inconvenienced who will appear, while others who would not be inconvenienced will decline.

Let it suffice to say that whatever the motivations are, finding a friendly bystander, who will agree to go to court as my witness is not a common occurrence. First, If I am cited for speeding on a freeway or major highway, there are not going to be any bystanders, friendly or otherwise, mailing a letter or waiting to cross the intersection that isn't there. Hitch hikers standing at the side of the road are probably not the best prospective witnesses for a variety of reasons. Second. If I am cited on a city street, the person mailing a letter or waiting to cross the intersection probably is not going to stay around or want to get involved in someone else's problem, regardless of how sympathetic they may be.

Chances are, if I am going to court with a witness, it will be someone who was in my car with me at the time I was cited.

It should come as no surprise to anyone that a witness who was in my vehicle with me when I was cited will be severely challenged by the prosecutor as being biased in my favor. Conversely, if there was another officer with the one who cited me, the prosecutor would want to represent him as an impartial professional whose expertise and recollections are above reproach or suspicion. It's reality.

Reality is what I have to deal with in court. Thus, I am very cautious about bringing witnesses to court and even more cautious about what I want the witness to testify to. I know my witness will be challenged. I know the prosecutor will try everything she can to discredit my witness and to confuse him or her to the point of giving an answer that will hurt my case.

This chapter deals with finding, selecting and determining whether to bring a witness to court. A later chapter will address witness testimony.

In the final analysis, whether or not I bring a witness or witnesses to court will be determined by who and how many witnesses may be available; the nature and type of citation; certain circumstances of the issuance of the citation, such as any specific act of outrageous or unprofessional behavior by the citing officer or anyone else; the issues to which a witness could testify; and, my sense of the witness' motivation (a witness who simply hates traffic officers would not be an asset).

Making the decision whether to use or not use a witness is a complex process requiring serious, penetrating analysis of the potential advantages and disadvantages. It is a decision I make with great care.

CHAPTER SIX

Delay..Delay..Delay.

The politics of postponement.

Some years ago, I was working as a licensed private investigator. I had plans to return to law school for my law degree and to run for the State Legislature. The underlying premise was that a State Legislator's law practice was assured because State Legislators get unlimited continuances in court for their cases. This was not a discovery I made on my own. The practice was common knowledge.

I spent a considerable amount of time in the courthouse during the time I was a P.I., waiting to testify in cases I was involved with. Perhaps the single most important thing I learned was that the key to success in most trials was the effectiveness of the delaying tactics employed by the winning attorney. It seemed to me that delay was the name of the game.

I decided, at some point that I did not want to be a lawyer. I did not want to be part of the problem. I spent so much time in courtrooms and hallways, while waiting to testify; hearing the deals being made between prosecutors and defense attorneys, discovering just how corrupt the whole system is, that I came to be repulsed by the idea of ever being a part of it.

I still believe we have the best system of justice in the world, here in America. However, I also believe the system is rotting. I believe we will lose this great nation of ours some day if we fail to fix all of the things that are wrong with our judicial system.

What I took away from my education about the court system, as it relates to the relatively insignificant issues of traffic court was that delay was a winning strategy.

Here again, the H word rears its ugly head. I have had a few people tell me I am a Hyprocrite for using delaying tactics to win my traffic cases. Their claim was that the delaying tactics are part of the corruption of the system that I so often criticize.
I cannot stand before God and everybody and state unequivocally that I have never done anything hypocritical. Perhaps I have, but I do not think so. My understanding of the term is that a hypocrite is one who intentionally pretends to hold a view that is societally correct, but actually doesn't; or is one who intends to deceive people by pretending to be something he or she is not. I try always to be genuine and sincere in all that I do.

I use any and every legitimate delay tactic I believe will help me win my traffic case in court because that is how the system is structured. It is part and parcel of the judicial system on every level. There are many practices which I think are wrong within the system. I believe, for example, that it is wrong to take money from a family because the breadwinner made an error while driving to work. But that is exactly what the system seeks to do. What's more, the system uses every heavy handed tactic you can think of to achieve that end, and then compounds the travesty by adding taxes and other surcharges on top of the fines.

I believe the traffic courts across this nation *as they are presently run*, are a massive *cancer* on our society. They are unfair, inefficient and hugely incompetent. The billions of dollars collected in traffic courts do little, **if anything**, that I can see to create better drivers or add anything to the real economy of the land. As I see them, the collective traffic courts of the nation exist and persist mainly for the purpose of perpetuating a counter-productive bureaucracy, *which produces nothing for society.*

I believe we need traffic laws and traffic courts - but not the kind we have today.

In any case, I do not believe it is hypocritical or wrong to use delaying tactics in traffic court. I do use such tactics and have been very successful doing so. Consider the following example.

During one period several years back, I received three citations for four violations. I was pulled over on the service road of a freeway by a motorcycle officer with a radar gun. He issued me a citation for driving 45 miles per hour in a 35 mile per hour zone. He may have been right about my speed. I am certain he had no trouble filling his quota at that location. The service road was bounded on the left by the freeway and on the right by several hundred acres of vacant, undeveloped land. The distance from the exit off the freeway to the first intersection was slightly more than half a mile.

A few weeks later, I was stopped after making a right turn on a red light. The officer said I did not come to a complete stop. I believe I did. I would also point out that there was no traffic in sight, coming from my left on the street into which I turned. The officer issued me a citation for failing to stop for a traffic light.

Two days later, I had the exhaust system on my car replaced; new engine pipe, muffler and tail pipe. About a mile from the muffler shop after I picked up my car, the engine pipe, which had not been properly secured to the muffler by the mechanic who did the work, separated from the muffler. The result was a very loud car. I immediately changed from the right lane to the left, planning to make a left turn and circle back to the muffler shop to see what was wrong.

As I started my left turn, I saw a police car. The cruiser had pulled out of the side street on what had been my right at the time my muffler separated. The officer flipped on his flashing lights and gunned his car up to my rear bumper as I completed my left turn. I pulled over and turned off the engine. There were two officers and both got out. They walked up to my car and recited the usual request for license and registration. I asked why he stopped me as I handed him my documents. "You have a defective muffler", he replied. "Well no", I said, "I have a brand new muffler that I just got this evening. I'm on my way back to the shop to see what's wrong." I don't know why he took such offense from my reply. I did not use a sarcastic tone with him or anything like that. "You also made an unsafe lane change", he barked at me.

Now, you might imagine that I was getting a little annoyed by then. You would be correct. I told the officer that I had just left the shop five minutes ago, having paid a substantial sum for a complete new exhaust system. I invited him to look under the car and see for himself. I also invited him to study my receipt. And I told him that I most certainly had not made an unsafe lane change. I had signalled and checked over my left shoulder to confirm that I had plenty of room for the lane change. I also pointed out to him that there was enough room behind me before I made the turn for him to have roared out of the side street and make the left turn on my rear bumper. At that point it became obvious that he was no longer my buddy. He wrote me up for a defective muffler and an unsafe lane change. Since it was clear we were no longer best buddies, I said "I'll see you in court".

In the space of a few weeks, I had a handful of tickets. The strategy I used was to get several continuances on the court dates. I was able to do that by dropping in at the court clerk's office a few days before the court date and give an excuse for why I would not be able to appear on that date. All three tickets had different dates, of course.
After receiving all the continuances I could get, my next move was to not show up in court. This event occurred several years ago and courts were more lenient than they are now. It requires

a different strategy now to avoid a penalty for failure to appear.

A few months after the ticket went to warrant, I received a phone call from the warrant officer informing me he had these warrants for my arrest and that I could avoid being arrested by going down to the court and paying the fines (entering a plea of guilty) or, posting cash bonds (ten dollars more than the fine amount) for the tickets and setting a trial date. I posted the cash bonds, set trial dates and got my receipts.

I set all of the tickets for the same trial date. Then, I was able to get three more continuances before I finally had to go to trial. On the trial date, none of the officers appeared in court. One of the officers (the red light ticket) had been promoted to detective. Detectives in that jurisdiction, at that time couldn't be called to traffic court. The judge was going to have to dismiss the ticket. He was not a happy man. He informed me that he was going to dismiss that ticket but that he would not dismiss the others. He reset them for two weeks hence.

Two weeks later I was back in court. Again, none of the officers showed up. The judge was very upset. The traffic school option was not available at that time in that jurisdiction (it still is not offered in some jurisdictions). I decided to be a little creative. I said, "Your honor, I would like to offer a solution that should be satisfactory to both of us. I would like to propose that you dismiss the defective muffler and unsafe turn ticket, since I am fully prepared to prove that both counts are wrong. Then, I would plead guilty to the 45 in a 35 ticket if, in exchange for my guilty plea you would sentence me to take a safe driving course, pay no fine and have the guilty plea set aside after I complete the course.

The judge gazed at me as if I had just arrived from another planet. "I can't agree to such a proposal", he said. "Of course you can, Judge", I replied. "You're the Judge. You can do as you please", I added. "Well I am not agreeing to such a plan. I am not favorably disposed to such a thing", he said. "Well, your honor, in that case, I have to with draw my offer and state that I am not guilty and I'm here, ready for trial', I said in the most respectful tone I could muster. "The officers are not available for trial today", he said. "I am resetting these cases". "With all due respect, you honor", I replied, "I don't think it's fair, but I'll be here ready for trial next time, too." The date was reset, again two weeks hence.

It came as no surprise to me that the officers did not show up again. I later learned that the motorcycle cop had retired. When my cases were called and the officers were not there, I demanded that It would be improper to reset them again and moved for dismissal on both tickets. The judge, reluctantly and unhappily, agreed and dismissed the cases. Perhaps the best part was that, in those days, there was a cashier in the courtroom, complete with a big cash register.

When you were found guilty, you paid your fine to the cashier, who rang up the big cash register and handed you a receipt.

But when you won your trial and had cash bonds posted, they refunded your money right there in the courtroom in front of God and everybody. They really hated to have to do that. I thought it was great, personally.

The story above certainly does not reflect a typical situation. Far from it. It was by far the most unusual victory by delaying tactics that I ever enjoyed. The potential for victory, however, has always been greatly enhanced for me by the application of all possible delaying tactics.

CHAPTER SEVEN

Early Motions.

The first opportunities for victory.

The day arrives; I appear in court at the prescribed time, ready for trial. When I arrive in court, I am primed. I have psyched myself up; used all of the techniques and tricks I know to get myself **UP** for the trial. I go into court **believing** I am better prepared than my adversaries; **confident** I am **going to win.**

The best possible outcome is to win my case before the prosecutor ever gets to put the officer on the stand to testify against me. It doesn't happen often. But it does happen. Let me illustrate some of the possibilities.

If I appear in court, ready for trial, and the officer is not there, I immediately move for dismissal. I inform the judge that I have appeared as I promised, when I signed the citation; that I had to make certain sacrifices to do so. I state emphatically that I am ready for trial and confident that my testimony, and the supporting evidence I can present, will result in a not guilty verdict. Finally; I insist that if I failed to appear the judge would issue a warrant for my arrest and fine me. Thus, because of the officer's failure to appear, my case should be dismissed.

Occasionally, the judge will immediately grant the motion to dismiss. More often, he will reply that he will give the officer some additional time to appear; that he will call the rest of the docket and then recall my case. If this happens, I will excuse myself and declare to the judge that putting my case back is an unfair hardship. I will have to miss more time from my work and lose more money, all because the officer did not place the same importance on appearing on time as I have, choosing instead to waste the court's time and mine. I will then repeat my motion to dismiss. This might result in the judge's reconsideration of the circumstances and his decision to dismiss.

If the judge does not reconsider and dismiss, I will respond by saying, "I respect your authority to rule as you are, Judge. But please note my exception, for the record." This statement puts the judge on notice that I did not just fall off the turnip truck; that I know I have rights and I'm not intimidated by the process. I have just respectfully informed the judge that I will use every means available to me to appeal my case, if necessary.

When my case is recalled at the end of the docket, it will most likely be dismissed if the officer still has not appeared. If the case is not dismissed, but re-set by the judge, I will again ask him to please note my exception for the record. This time, though, I will add, "And please note my intention to appeal in the event of a decision unfavorable to me."

My declaration at this point, that I will appeal if I ultimately lose, may annoy the judge. He may bristle at what he perceives as my gall. (Whom do I think I am talking to?) On the other hand, he may show some degree of amusement at my declaration. (Who does this amateur think he is kidding?) Either way, it makes no difference to me. I do know this much: my declaration will probably get him thinking about whether it was wise to continue a case when the officer did not show up. He may reflect on my declaration for a moment or two and decide not to invite the aggravation of a later appeal or a risk of reversal. No judge wants to be reversed, ever. He just may be detached and objective enough at the moment to say. "Okay, your case is dismissed. You may go." It's hard to predict these things. But if I do persist –

respectfully - I may give him just the additional motivation he may need to decide not to be bothered any further.

I will make a motion to dismiss, as soon as my case is called, if there is any defect in the citation. I will move for dismissal on the grounds that the citation is improperly drawn, citing the defect or defects. A defect in the citation is, in fact, grounds for dismissal in many, perhaps all, jurisdictions. That does not guarantee the judge will dismiss. If the judge resists; offers some excuse for the officer's error, perhaps it is because he harbors some sort of personal bias against people, like me, who appear before him confident and assured, sans the usual nervousness and trembling exhibited by many, if not most, of the defendants he sees.

My experience has shown that many judges do not like to see defendants feeling sure of themselves, challenging the system (as they see it) that is structured to intimidate them, usurping the turf of the lawyers and demanding their rights. A smaller number of judges appear to be impartial to, or at least tolerant of such defendants. A few judges I have seen appeared to welcome such a defendant as a refreshing change in the usual routine, even to the point of dispensing a compliment or two on the defendant's preparation and/or knowledge.

If the judge refuses to dismiss, I will put him on notice of my exception and my intent to appeal in the event of an unfavorable outcome. Judges do not like to be reversed on appeal. Many judges, though, are so full of themselves; they don't think for a moment that some common layman could win a reversal against them. Some lessons get learned the hard way. Yes, even by judges, who ought to know better.

I do not rely on having my early motions granted. My primary purpose for making these motions (aside from the occasional on the spot victory) is to provide a basis for appeal. I believe, also, that making these motions accomplishes two more significant things. First, it shows the judge, the prosecutor, and the officer that I am a few clicks above their usual adversary. Second, it helps to undermine the confidence and concentration of the officer and the prosecutor, increasing the possibility one of them will make an error helping my case.

There is yet one other, rather subtle, benefit to me derived from making these early motions. As I offer my motions and respond to the replies from the judge, the verbal volleying captures the attention of the people in the courtroom. Things become quieter as first a few, then more and more people become interested in the exchange of words. In my experience, my stature becomes elevated in the eyes of those assembled. The net effect of that is a further erosion of the officer's concentration on the task before him. No, I am not suffering from delusions of grandeur. It is a very subtle thing. It doesn't change me, except perhaps to help me feel more confident and relaxed. But, take my word for it. It does further undermine the concentration of the officer, and the prosecutor, as well.

Now we will revisit the San Diego Freeway Caper I introduced in Chapter One. You will recall that I was denied my right to have the citation answerable in the central court at the County seat. I appeared at the South County Court at the appointed time and immediately moved for dismissal when my case was called, citing the fact that I was denied due process under the law. I recited the section of the vehicle code and explained to the court that the section entitles me to have the citation answerable at the County seat. I told the judge that I had specifically, repeatedly, and emphatically told the officer I wanted the citation drawn accordingly, and that he refused to do so.

The judge seemed to be a little confused and said he was unfamiliar with that section of the vehicle code. He went on to say that I was here now and might as well go ahead with the case. I told the judge I didn't wish to do that. I said I believed trying the case in South Court gave the officer an unfair advantage and in any event, I was entitled to have the case tried at the County Seat. My insistence did not sit well with my friend the judge. He obviously did not often encounter what he probably considered such impertinent behavior from a lowly defendant in his court.

With an impatient wave of his arm, the judge said he "didn't have time for this business and was not granting any motion to dismiss." I believe the judge thought I would fall into line at that point. His error! As the judge was about to continue speaking, probably planning to tell the prosecutor to call his witness, I again spoke out. "Excuse me, your honor", I said. "In light of your refusal to grant my motion to dismiss, I must now move for a change of venue, based on the same vehicle code citation I made in my previous motion."

At that point, his facial expression, body language and tone of voice made it crystal clear that this judge did not like me or my persistence in this matter. "I've never heard of such a thing", he said. "I don't even know how we could set up something like that". I spoke up again. "Your honor, if you plan to deny this motion, too, then please understand that I will ask you to disqualify yourself on the grounds that I perceive that you hold some kind of prejudice against me". There is, or at least there was at the time, a statute in California that required a judge to step aside if the statute was invoked. The defendant only had to cite his own belief of the judge's prejudice.

The courtroom had become quiet earlier in our exchange. The silence had become complete. The judge clearly appeared to be provoked. However, I was meticulous in both the selection of my words and, perhaps more importantly, my tone of voice. I made a total effort to show respect for the judge, while firmly standing my ground. Judges have power. I did not wish to be held in contempt and, indeed, I was doing nothing to warrant such a move. I have had judges threaten me with contempt, though, when I was guilty of no such behavior.

The judge spoke out to his clerk, calling her by name and asking if she knew what they would have to do to set up a change of venue. She did not. Then, the judge turned to me and said, "You may go. I will have the clerk do whatever what must be done to arrange a change of venue to the Central Court. You'll be notified."

Bang! Just like that, I had the victory I came for. I believe the judge had a victory of sorts as well. Remember, it was the officer, not the judge who denied my rights. Clearly, I did not make the judge's day. He was smart enough, though, and professional enough, to recognize that he was being drawn into a situation that could come back to haunt him. He made the smart move; the right decision. I believe his change of venue paperwork was probably accompanied by some margin notes about me to the next judge. But that's fair.

I will relate all of the remaining details of the San Diego Freeway Caper in a later chapter. In closing this chapter, the point I want to establish with crystal clarity is that there are numerous possibilities for early motions, depending upon the circumstances of the case. I do my homework; search for every possible early motion that can help me win. With carefully scripted early motions I may gain an immediate victory or establish a basis for a win later in trial, or on appeal.

CHAPTER EIGHT

Exhibits and Physical Evidence.

A picture...or an object...worth the proverbial thousand words

More and more, we live in a visually oriented society. When I was a child we did not have television. We listened to radio programs and had to use our own imaginations to visualize the action we were hearing.

I recall an experience I had when I was a young boy. There was a radio program on Saturday mornings called "Let's Pretend". The program was a great kids' favorite. I was thrilled when the opportunity came to see one of the live broadcasts in the studio. I was wild with anticipation for the week I had to wait. When Saturday finally arrived and we took the subway to Manhattan to get to the studio, I was really excited. Well, I can't begin to describe how disappointed I was by the end of the program. All of the excitement was replaced by a feeling of what I can best describe as loss. In the studio, I watched the three cast members read the parts of five characters into the microphones. I sat with my eyes riveted on the sound effects man as he created all of the sounds that would have seemed so authentic at the other end of the airwaves, but sounded so false, as the sound effects man created them, using all sorts of gadgets and materials. All of the magic; all of the real enjoyment of the story vanished. It was not any fun. The program, and most of the other programs I usually listened to, never again had the same spellbinding effect on me.

Then television came along and nothing has been the same since. Today, neither kids nor adults want to use their own imaginations to visualize a scene or event. They want to actually see the event. Indeed, I believe, many kids and adults today cannot muster the imagery skills to mentally visualize things as people everywhere once did as routinely as tying their shoes.

The old saying "a picture is worth a thousand words" has always been true. It is truer than ever today. Thus, if I can appear in court, prepared to show a picture, or several pictures, or one or more objects that will support my case, I am increasing my odds of victory. Bringing photos or other physical objects to court produced an even greater result when I could still have my traffic case tried before a jury. Judges are just as visually stimulated and conditioned as everyone else. But they tend to lean too far away from acceptance of what the physical exhibits show, perhaps because they do not want to be seen as easily swayed.

Nevertheless, it remains true that pictures and/or other physical objects with a connection to my traffic citation do provide an added dimension to my case and improve my prospects for victory. Interestingly enough, I have never seen an officer produce a picture or other physical object during his testimony against a defendant. I firmly believe in playing the percentages. If I can employ an element in my case that the other side does not have, I will.

If I get a ticket for an improper turn, for example, I can try to show evidence, in a photo, that the sign prohibiting the turn was completely obscured by an overgrowth of vegetation. or some other obstruction. The picture will show that I, or any other driver, would have been prevented from seeing the sign or, at least, of *seeing the sign in time to comply.* My case is strengthened. In order for me to obey such a traffic sign, it must be visible to me. Moreover, it must be visible from enough of a distance to enable me to obey it. If, because of the obstruction, I am able to see the sign only after halfway completing the turn, the sign does not meet the criteria that must be met under various statutes. I will win the case. If not in trial, I will win on appeal.

A substantial degree of the benefit of a picture or object, presented in evidence, rests not so much in the actual object itself or the scene portrayed, as in the effect it can have on the witness against you. What is important is the extent to which the picture or object affects the witness' ability to present her testimony. In other words, a carefully timed and wisely introduced, picture or object may so rattle the officer or other witness that he or she may stumble, make obvious errors, to be stretching the truth or even lying.

Once again, from my experience, it appears that most judges will cut a lot of slack for the officer or other witness in testimony that is in conflict with pictorial or other physical evidence, not wanting to put too much weight on the photo or object. However, even in a situation where the judge behaves in a manner which ignores the true weight of the evidence, I believe he is psychologically helpless to ignore it completely. The end result, in trial, is that my opponent's testimony will be diminished *to some degree* by the photo or object in evidence, giving me an advantage I would not have without it.

It is also noteworthy that any physical evidence I intend use in trial must have a **direct bearing** or **connection** to the citation and/or the charges covered by it. Photos of the scene must be photos that were made as close to the time the citation was issued as possible. And I must be able to prove when the photos were taken.

One thing I usually do is; after I get the film developed at a one hour photo processing shop, I place the photos in an envelope and mail them to myself, leaving the envelope sealed until I get to court. I can thus prove that the photos were not taken after the date of the postmark. Obviously, I would have had no reason to take such photos **before** receiving the citation. Therefore, I can reasonably establish that the photos accurately depict the conditions at the site of the citation on the day I received it - provided of course that I take and develop the pictures on that day.

In the case I refer to as the San Diego Freeway Caper, a physical object played a major role in my case. I used the object to great advantage in my cross-examination of the officer. The object was central to a point I wanted to firmly establish; that the officer **made a mistake.** The object would support my claim that the officer made a fundamental error and that, confronted with the evidence to show him his error, he chose to pursue a false course to justify issuing the citation.

Though the ultimate outcome of the case did not rest directly on the object I entered into evidence, I believe it clearly, and rightly, cast serious doubt on the officer's testimony. Ultimately, had the outcome not been the result of a series of other, more compelling issues, the object may have been even more of a factor and the basis of a victorious outcome.

The point to focus on is that using such evidence as pictures or other physical objects in trial makes perfect sense. It gives me the potential for great advantage with virtually no downside. I like that. Having an advantage over one's opponent in a battle is a huge confidence builder.

CHAPTER NINE

The Traffic Officer's Testimony.

I listen and learn....

At the point when the prosecutor calls the officer to the witness stand, all of my primary sources for motions to dismiss will have been addressed and ruled upon, e.g. motion to dismiss due to defects in the citation, etc. My focus, at this point, is to listen intently to the officer's testimony, make concise notes (written notes) of any and every statement the officer makes that is contrary to, or inaccurately reflects, what actually happened at the scene when the citation was issued.

I have stated elsewhere that police officers, prosecutors and judges are just people, human beings like all the rest of us. They are subject to the same ambitions, limitations, faults, and lapses in character as everyone else on the planet. Will a policeman lie on the witness stand; give false testimony against me? That is an interesting question; an important question. It took a long time for me to **resolve** that question in my own mind. Here's what I mean.

Instinctively, the answer I came up with was, "Of course the officer would lie". I could answer the question instantly. Then, a funny thing happened. **Doubt** sneaked into my brain and found its way to my ear. Why would the officer lie? Why would he give false testimony against me? What could be in it for him? He would need some motivation to lie.

All of these questions associated with the doubt that had filtered into my thought process clouded my thinking and caused me to lose focus on what I should have been doing. The struggle going on inside my head so distracted me that my ability to analyze the officer's testimony and pinpoint certain words and phases in his answers to the prosecutor's questions suffered. By extension, my ability to conduct an effective and efficient cross examination of the officer also suffered, reducing my chances of victory and increasing the risk of losing my family's financial resources.

At some point, I finally realized that I had to resolve the doubt issue in my own mind, once and for all. I studied the question more closely. "Would an officer lie on the stand; give false testimony against me?" By intently studying the question, I came to realize that there was really more to it, buried in my subconscious. The question, as I came to understand, was also: "Would the Prosecutor conspire with the officer to construct a story that would insure a conviction?" Furthermore, "Would the Judge do anything to deny me my rights? Would he try to cover up his own mistake, if he made one that I could use to secure victory?"

I am what some people call a voracious reader. I read everything. I read labels, directions, The Bible, books of every type and description, magazines, trade and professional journals, marketing, advertising and promotional pieces, junk mail, billboards, bulletin boards, personal correspondence, you name it. If it is in print, either on paper or an electronic format of some kind, and finds its way to a point within my peripheral range of vision, I will read it. I have, more than once, been caught red handed reading...*instructions*, of all things. In finding the answer to the questions I have cited above, I went deep inside my own head. I called upon the entire body of knowledge I have accumulated over my entire life, as well as my memory and recollections of all of the events of my life.

Finally, I came to that breakthrough point, at which everything settles into place and a clear understanding emerges, like the brightest star in the sky. "Yes" ***was, and is***, the answer. The officer, the prosecutor, the judge; any or all of them could, and under certain circumstances would, lie or commit some other act that would deny my rights, ensure victory for their side and take money from my family.

To give you an idea of some of the proofs I presented to myself in my search for that answer, here are a couple of examples: Has any person, deemed by society to be a great individual, one who may have made thousands of positive contributions to society and mankind, ever been found guilty of a criminal act? Did Peter the Chief Apostle of Jesus Christ; whom Peter had declared to be his Lord and Savior, deny three times, on the night before the crucifixion of Jesus, that he knew the man? It was important for me to convince myself that the officer, the prosecutor or the judge could lie or commit some other illegal or unethical act to win. It was important to remove the doubt that lingered in my mind; to clearly establish that it was not just me, saying it could happen.

I have passed the milestone; completely eliminated all doubt from my mind. Having done so does not mean that I now believe the officer is **going to lie**. But now I can, and do, focus completely on constructing my case.

As the officer answers each of the prosecutor's questions, I write down my notes and key words or phases to use in my cross-examination of the officer. Frequently, the prosecutor will simply ask the officer to tell the court the circumstances and details of the citation, allowing the officer to simply recite his notes.

Whatever tactics the prosecutor employs in directing the officer's testimony, I make copious notes. I note even the smallest deviation from the actual conditions or circumstances that existed at the time and place I was cited. I construct my notes in a specific outline format, so I can incorporate them into the cross-examination outline I have already prepared prior to the trial.

Depending upon the nature of the ticket; the offense cited, location, time, etc., I will have constructed my cross- examination outline to address certain specific items. Such as: where my car was when first observed by the officer, where he was, what brought my vehicle to his attention, the distances between us, how many other vehicles, and of what types were present in the immediate vicinity.

Thus, when the officer has completed his direct testimony, I have additional points to use on cross-examination; all identified and labeled to fit into my cross examination outline structure.

...then, I attack on cross.

There was a time when I was nervous about cross-examining the officer. Like all of us, I had been pre-conditioned by the system to be intimidated by the entire traffic court process. It was as though challenging the officer was some sort of sacrilegious act. I learned quickly to overcome that foolish notion and developed my cross-examination skills to enable me to zero in on the weak spots of the officer's testimony and strengthen my case.

Almost always, the officer will have made a mistake of some kind. The outline I prepare for my cross-examination of the officer is structured to uncover as many of the officer's errors as I can. Some of the mistakes I uncover may do nothing more than undermine the officer's credibility regarding certain aspects of the events related to the citation. Most judges I have observed will tend to be relatively unmoved when I am able to reveal some weaknesses in the credibility of the officer's testimony. Therefore, it is important for me to persist in my search for errors; to methodically chip away at each and every weakness until there is nothing else to challenge.

In the course of revealing errors made by the officer, I am always searching for the "mother lode"; a statement in which he clearly contradicts his earlier testimony; better yet, an admission by the officer that he has broken a rule or violated a law himself in his performance.

Consider the following: the prosecutor tells the court he has no further questions of the witness. The officer's direct testimony is finished; complete. The judge asks me if I have any questions I would like to ask the officer. Usually, the judge is not prepared for what follows. He or she will rarely expect to see a defendant before him who is not only un-intimidated, but prepared and organized. Of course, my diligent note taking during the officer's testimony provides the judge with an indication this will not be a run of the mill traffic case. The judge's attention level will jump a few clicks when I respond, enthusiastically, in the most up-beat tone of voice I can manage. "Yes indeed, your honor, I have a number of questions for this officer to answer", I reply, fixing my attention on the officer, looking him straight in the eye.

I always offer a broad smile and offer a friendly greeting to the officer, first. "Hello, Officer Smith, how are you today?" My greeting is not a simple exercise of my social graces. First, I want the judge to take note of the fact that I am a civilized, educated person, who exhibits no hostility or disrespect toward the officer. Second, my greeting has a disarming effect upon the officer. I want him to relax and drop his guard a bit.

For a long time, offering a broad smile to the officer was something I could not manage very well. I was, after all, not happy with him or the possibility of having to give away some of my hard earned money. I overcame the problem by taking a few moments to reflect on the fact that I am convinced I will prevail. I will win, I will remind myself just as I prepare to flash my smile and greet the officer. Then I will begin my questioning, taking my time, carefully arranging my notes and outline papers. If I have any physical exhibits I plan to use, they will also be carefully arranged, close at hand.

"Officer Smith", I will begin, "on the day of such and such date, when you issued me a citation for exceeding the maximum speed (quoting here the language actually written on the citation in the Offense space), where was my vehicle, when you first observed it?" The officer may consult his notebook or may answer without doing so. I will check my own notes to see if his answer agrees with mine. If his answer doesn't agree with my own notes, I will make an entry in the appropriate section of my outline for my own testimony. Then, I will challenge the officer's answer or wait until he answers my next question. Next, I will ask him where his own vehicle was, at the time he first observed mine. Again, I will check his answer against my own notes.

I have an advantage in this exchange. Although the officer has his notebook with the notes he made immediately after writing my citation, he probably did not think, at the time, that I would also prepare notes; more detailed than his own. He also probably did not put a high probability on my appearing in court to try the case.

My experience has been that the officer did not make any notation of where each of us were at the time he first observed my vehicle, beyond something like "southbound on I-405". His response to my first question may be vague. He may simply say that I was driving south on I-405. In that case, I will press him for a more specific answer, until he either says I was in lane such and such, fifty yards ahead of him or admits he does not recall exactly where I was.

The questions and answers continue until I have testimony from him of the precise location of both vehicles, or his admission that he can't recall. By the end of this initial exchange of questions and answers, the officer will almost always be on the defensive.

Often, the officer will bluff. He will glance at his notes and rattle off an answer about the location of the vehicle or vehicles that I know to be wrong from my own notes. When that happens, I will comment on it. I may say something like,"I see you consulted your notes for the answer to my question. Would you care to read from those notes and tell the court exactly what you wrote?"

If he is bluffing, he has a problem. If he pretends to read something from his notes that isn't there, the content of his notes then becomes testimony and I will ask him to show those notes to the court and me. If he then retreats from his testimony and tries to cancel out his false reading, saying something like, "Well I wasn't actually reading my notes themselves. I was just recalling things, by looking through what I have here." he has just been caught in a lie and his performance on the stand from that point forward will be all downhill.

I will not call the officer a liar. I will not ask him if he is lying. I will use body language; subtle gestures (a slight downward tilt of my chin accompanied by a very slight shake of my head). I will make eye contact with the officer and hold it for a few moments. My facial expression as I hold my attention on the officer, maintaining eye contact will be one of disappointment; the kind of look I would show to an old friend who had betrayed me. Then I will turn my head slightly toward the judge and for just a fleeting moment make eye contact and quickly break it off.

I learned from experience that a court trial; any court trial, must include the use of a certain amount of theatrics. The showmanship and theatrical ability possessed by a trial lawyer will, to a great extent, determine his level of success. When I am trying my traffic case, I am my own trial lawyer. I have never agreed with the old adage that "Anyone who serves as his own attorney, and represents himself in court, has a fool for a client" nor have I applied it in trying my own traffic cases in court. First of all, I am not an attorney. Secondly, most of the lawyers I've seen trying traffic cases wouldn't do half the job I do. I believe having a lawyer try your case for a traffic violation works against you in the eyes of the court. Lastly, the cost of hiring an attorney and winning would probably exceed the cost of losing the case on your own.

My next series of questions for the officer will focus on the details of the other vehicles around me; their numbers, placement, relative speeds, and the like. The object of these questions is to further show that the quality of the officer's testimony is poor.

At some point in the cross-examination, I will ask the officer about calibrations. If the citation was based on the use of a radar gun or similar apparatus, I will ask the officer for the details of the calibration procedure for the instrument. I will ask when the instrument was last calibrated, prior to the officer citing me. I will then ask when it was next calibrated after, I was cited. The calibration I am referring to here is not the day to day field calibration the officer does, but the periodic factory or laboratory calibration which is prescribed for the unit.

If the officer stopped me as the result of having paced me, using his vehicle's speedometer, I will ask for the same information regarding calibrations of his vehicle's speedometer.

After the officer has testified to the dates of the calibrations of either his radar gun or his speedometer, I will then probe more deeply. I will ask for copies of the **certified calibration reports** of the instrument or the speedometer. Once the officer has given testimony that the calibrations were conducted on such and such dates, he must be able to prove that his testimony is truthful. He must be able to provide independent evidence attesting to the accuracy of his testimony. Thus, I will then ask the officer to present the certified calibrations into evidence. My experience has been that the officer usually does not have the documents with him and will not be able to offer them into evidence.

Few judges would recess a trial for the time it would take the officer to return to his station, retrieve the documents and bring them back to court. I do know of one judge, however, who did precisely that. No. Actually, the individual I refer was not actually a judge, but a "Judge Pro-tem". A Judge Pro-tem is an attorney appointed to act as a Judge in the absence of enough real judges to handle court case loads. I do not know how widespread the practice of using "Pro-tem" judges is. But it is, or at least once was routinely done in certain jurisdictions in California. I do not know if the person I have referred to above ever became a real judge, but you will learn more about my experience with him later in this chapter.

Now, let's go back to cross-examining the officer. If the officer can not produce the certified calibrations for his radar unit or speedometer, as may be the case, I will then move for dismissal. The grounds for my motion are that there is no documented evidence before the court to show that the radar unit or speedometer, which is the basis for the charge in the citation, has in fact ever been calibrated, as the law requires.

I will remind the judge that the officer's testimony concerning calibrations is not substantiated by any kind of factual documentation and, therefore, must be treated as hearsay. No one but me, and any other "Defendants-in-waiting" remaining in the courtroom, will like my motion. The officer and prosecutor will no doubt show their appropriate horror and indignation at the suggestion that the officer is not telling the truth, though no such suggestion has been made. The judge may also be somewhat upset over the motion that seems to be saying the officer's testimony cannot be trusted, though no one has actually said so.

You see, the problem in all of this is that the people who operate the traffic court system, at least some of them, really do not want to be held to the lofty standards imposed on courts by the Constitution of the United States, or of their own State Constitution. Many of these folks do not support the idea of providing the traffic court defendant a level playing field upon which to engage his adversary. It is, nevertheless, true that the prosecution – even in a mere traffic case – has the responsibility to prove the charge in the citation.

It follows, that if a radar unit or a speedometer was the instrument used to bring the charge in the citation, then the prosecution must be required to **prove** that the instrument was calibrated and certified, as statutorily required. I believe most states have detailed statutory requirements for the frequency and specific procedures of calibrating and *certifying* those instruments.

It is my own responsibility to research the law, find and familiarize myself with the details of the statute. I also believe, however, that I can win my case with, or without such a statute on the books, if not in court, then on appeal. My motion will almost certainly set off a spirited, even heated verbal free-for-all. The prosecutor may try to make much of the fact that the officer conducts a field calibration procedure on the unit every time he uses it, or at the beginning of every shift.

Such a field calibration, though, does not truly attest to the accuracy of the instrument. An **anecdotal analogy** I like to use . . . and I have used it several times in court, is the one about a man who worked at an Army Base. One of the duties of his job was to fire the cannon at the Base Gate each morning at exactly eight o'clock. Each morning, on his way to work, he would calibrate his wristwatch to the imposing tower clock in front of the city's most prestigious jewelry store.

He took his watch to that shop one day to have it cleaned and serviced. He believed in good preventative maintenance. As the master jeweler worked on his watch, the man told the jeweler how much he admired the tower clock in front of the store. The jeweler thanked him and went on to say, with pride, that the clock had lost only one second in the preceding five years. The man was quite impressed and asked what kind of calibration procedure the jeweler used to maintain the clock's accuracy. "Well", said the jeweler," you see, every morning, at eight o'clock sharp, they fire a cannon out at the army base".

As the old saying goes, "things are not always what they seem."

Allow me to add just one more note about getting the analogy above into the testimony. Though I have succeeded in getting it in on several occasions, I have also been abruptly shut down by the Judge more than once. Some Judges are more astute than others. Some judges are more patient than others and some, more impatient. You get the idea. But understand that getting the analogy in cripples any attempt to elevate a field calibration to a substitute for a certified calibration. If the judge allows such a tactic he creates a clear basis for appeal.

My motion may be granted, or not. If not, then at least I have strong ammunition for my appeal. Need I say that if my motion is denied, I will most certainly; firmly request that the judge note my exception *for the record* and put him on notice that I will appeal.

The point of the references I make here to the cross-examination of the officer is to thoroughly and methodically attack his testimony, to pick it apart and reveal its inaccuracy, to devalue it to the point that it does not hurt me.

Another thing I want to mention in connection with hearing the testimony of the officer and cross-examining him. I go to court with a total plan. Part of that plan is my script for my own testimony, which comes later. In hearing the officer's testimony and cross-examining him, I will try to steer him and get him to give answers that will add punch to my own testimony later.

Two things I keep crystal clear in my mind to help me get the most out of cross-examining the officer are these: First, I never lose sight of the fact that I am engaged in an adversarial struggle which requires my opponent to lose, if I am to win. Thus, I must keep focused on making my opponent lose, by whatever means are available to me. Second, I never show even the smallest hint of disrespect to any of my opponents; I see the prosecutor, the officer and any witnesses against me as my opponents.

I may well show signs of being disappointed in one or all of them, through words, gestures or body language, but not in a way that comes across as being disrespectful of them. Neither do I go to extremes with respectfulness. If I have to dismantle the officer's testimony and reveal his mistakes and poor judgment; and I must if I am to win, I try to conduct that exercise in the manner of an older brother who has caught his younger brother in a bad situation. The older brother must expose the younger brother's transgression or failure, but do it in a way that tells the youngster that big brother is very disappointed in him, but knows little brother didn't mean to do it and will be good next time.

Yes, I am serious. And, yes, it takes practice to pull it off without being condescending. But it gets easier with practice . . . which reminds me of the story about the concert violinist about to make his debut at Carnegie Hall in New York. He is lost and can't find the place. With time getting very short he stops and asks an old, distinguished looking Armenian Peddler, "Sir, how do I get to Carnegie Hall?" The old man looks him in the eye and says, "Practice . . . Practice."

To further illustrate the points of this chapter, let me take you, once again, back to the San Diego Freeway Caper.

After a long delay, I finally did appear in Central Court in Santa Ana, the change of venue having been sent from South Court, no doubt with considerable margin notes encouraging the new judge to knock some of the wind out of my sails.

The new judge was a woman who was known to have high ambitions. Indeed, she did go on to higher courts and has conducted some high profile major trials. When my case was called, the officer was not present. I made my customary motion for dismissal on the grounds of the officer's failure to appear. The judge shot me an icy glare and I knew this was going to be anything but pleasant.

The judge asked the prosecutor where the officer was. I heard the prosecutor respond that the officer was not in court and was still in San Clemente, as far as he knew. The judge told the prosecutor to call down to San Clemente and send for the officer.

At that point, I spoke up. "Your Honor", I said, "I have other things to do today. The officer was supposed to be here, just as I was. This Officer does not respect the system. He refused to set this court as the place I had to answer his citation, as he is required to do under section 40502 of the vehicle code, which caused me to have to secure a change of venue, and" . . . "I know all about your change of venue trick, Sir", the judge interrupted. "And you got your change of venue. And you will have a seat and wait until the officer appears. Then you will have your day in court."

"Your Honor", I replied, "You are treating me unfairly. Had I not shown up here this morning you would have immediately issued a bench warrant for my arrest. But I did appear as required and I am ready for trial. Since the other side is not ready for trial, I must once again move for dismissal." "I'll tell you what you are going to do, Sir", the judge said angrily, "You are going to have a seat right over there in the jury box and wait for the officer to drive up here from San Clemente. Then we will hear this case, is that clear?"

I was steamed - mostly by the judge's imperious attitude and tone of voice. The word "snotty" comes to mind. There was no doubt in my mind that **she** had in mind teaching me a lesson: not to take on the system. "Very well then, Your Honor, I'll take a seat. But please note my exception and also please note that this is only another point, on a growing list of points, on which I will appeal if I do not prevail here today, Ma'am" "That will be all from you", she *shouted* at me, startling everyone in the courtroom. "I don't want to hear another word from you until I ask you to speak"

I feel certain the good judge was baiting me, hoping I would add another word or two. She would have held me in contempt, fined me, and probably stuck me in the cooler for several hours as well. I did not take the bait. Instead, I took a seat in the empty jury box to cool my heels until the officer arrived from San Clemente, thirty or so miles down the freeway.

BEFORE I CONTUINUE to relate the details of the San Diego Caper trial, it is important that I digress here a bit for a little aside. I want to highlight a few points, that relate to the ingredients which I believe make up the recipe for a successful outcome in traffic court. I'll call them "trace elements". There will be no test at the conclusion of this little aside. Nevertheless, I encourage you to follow along closely. Understanding these subtle trace elements is perhaps the most important aspect of how I win in traffic court.

Consider:

- The Central Court judge's overt hostility toward me was not the least bit surprising. I knew, when I forced the South Court judge into granting the change of venue, there was a strong likelihood I would not be welcomed to Central Court by a smiling, friendly judge. I have never known a judge who did not have a substantial ego. Nor have I ever met or known a judge who did not always try to maintain a certain degree of control in his or her relationships, both in and outside of court. The margin notes that probably accompanied the change of venue papers to Central Court likely described me as a renegade; someone who believed it was okay to challenge a judge's authority. Okay, I can handle that.

- I have said it before. I will go on saying, again, and again, and again, judges are only people. People with power, true enough, judges are. But the powers judges have are not supernatural. Having the powers of his or her office, a wall covered with diplomas and advanced degrees and a host of other credentials of this sort or the other, does not necessarily make judge Doe smarter than me.

- The truth, as I see it, is that traffic court is not, as the saying goes, rocket science. Traffic court is a place where matters relating to a relatively small number of laws are contested. All of the contests in traffic court must result in decisions proscribed by that relatively small body of laws. We all know, or should know that those very laws are all written down in public documents, available to us all, if we simply seek them out. There are no secret laws to reach out and catch us by surprise in traffic court.

- Indeed, there are numerous traffic laws on the books, throughout the nation, which are little known to police officers, prosecutors, judges and the general public because they are so seldom used. Such obscure little laws can be of great importance to one who searches for and finds them. The law that gave me the right to demand that the traffic citation I received far from home be made answerable in the central court of the County Seat is such a law. I will tell you why.

- First, consider for a moment the numerous benefits that law provides to me. It saves me from having to drive a long distance from my home to some remote corner of the county, (which could be close to a hundred miles in some cases) to a court where the judge, prosecutor and officer are all part of the local good buddy network. Instead, the officer would be the one to make the long drive and be as much a stranger in the courthouse as I am. That helps to level the playing field, one way or another. I'll explain what I mean by that.

- If the officer is one of the enlightened, and fills out the citation as the law requires, he will not be on his home turf, surrounded by the familiar faces of his good old boys. That is, if he shows up in court at all. The officer could play games with the law, as the officer in my San Diego Caper case did, refusing to make the citation answerable at the Central Court. His improper action provided me with valuable ammunition for powerful pre-trial motions based upon questions of law, which could later serve as the basis for a winning appeal.

- If you study what I have described to you thus far about my pre-trial motions and what they produced, one thing should stand out. The first judge was hacked at my motions, but managed to recover his cool and ship the case out. The officer, though he was smart enough to keep his mouth shut, was miffed that the judge gave in on the change of venue. The Central Court judge to whom the case was sent, surely with encouragement to toss the book at me, was steamed at having the case dumped in her lap, and even more steamed by my own unrelenting calls for dismissal. So what common thread stands out ?

- All of my opponents succumbed to anger and suffered major injury to their concentration. Keep in mind, also, that the prosecutors in both courts, though they did not participate in the official proceedings up to that point, suffered similar injury to their concentration. And the Trial has not yet even begun!

- Add to everything else the inescapable fact that the parties who will comprise my opposing team are an un-organized group of strangers to each other except, perhaps, the judge and prosecutor. On the other hand, I am prepared. I have done my groundwork, developed a plan with numerous contingencies covered. I have a script; a written outline. Before the trial is over, I will have my three adversaries at each other. In the end, I will win. I will work the three of them against each other. I know I will win, be it in court at the trial, or on appeal.

- I said before there are no secret laws to catch you by surprise in traffic court. But I have armed myself with a few surprises that will get me over the top. They have nothing to surprise me with. Knowing as I wait for the officer to arrive for trial, the surprises I have in store, makes it difficult for me to keep from grinning.

- I will conclude this little aside with these words: All of my actions, all of my words, before and during the trial, will be carefully orchestrated to turn my opponents against each other, to destroy their concentration, to provoke them to anger and to cause them to make mistakes. In the midst of all of that, I will, at the appropriate time, present my personal testimony and show convincing evidence that I am innocent of the charge. Through it all, I will stick with my plan and keep firmly in my mind the fact that I am better prepared than my adversaries and will win because of that.

Let me bring you back now to the San Diego caper. After a wait of about two hours, during which time the judge disposed of her calendar and took care of some other business, I was told the court would be in recess for lunch and the officer would be in court when we resumed at one o'clock. I saw no point in giving the judge my opinion of her decision and simply nodded my head to acknowledge that we would resume at one o'clock.

I returned to the courtroom at about twelve forty-five to get settled in. The courtroom was locked and I had to wait in the corridor. But I did use the time to review my game plan and get myself psyched up for the game. At one twenty-five, the bailiff unlocked the door and I entered the courtroom to find the prosecutor and the officer deep in discussion with the judge. I took a seat and waited for another five minutes or so until they concluded their meeting. The judge called the case and I walked to the Defense table and, along with the officer, was sworn and took my seat.

The prosecutor called the officer and asked him to relate the details of the citation. The officer, glancing from time to time at his notebook, went on to tell how he had observed me making a lane change on the southbound 405 freeway and exceeding the maximum speed. He told the court he moved in behind me and paced me doing seventy-two miles per hour. He said he then initiated a traffic stop and issued me a citation for exceeding the maximum speed. The prosecutor asked the officer what the maximum speed was in the area. I never did figure out what the point of asking that question was. Everyone knew the posted maximum speed wad fifty-five miles per hour.

I expected the prosecutor to ask some questions of the officer regarding the officer's failure to comply with section 40502, making the citation answerable at the county seat. I felt they had surely cooked up some justification for that, to take the curse off. I was surprised. The prosecutor did not mention anything about the issue. More startling than that, the prosecutor announced, "I have no further questions for the officer, you Honor". I sat in stunned silence until the judge, glaring at me asked, "Do you have any questions for the officer?" I had to shake myself to re-focus.

"Yes, your Honor, I have a number of questions for the officer", I replied. "Very well then, you may ask your questions", she said. I gathered my notes and methodically placed them in the order I wanted them and put the brown paper bag I had with me in place on the desk where I wanted it (it contained a couple of items of physical evidence I would use). I looked directly into the eyes of the judge and said, "Thank you, you Honor". "Yes, Officer Smith" (not his real name), I said, turning my head slightly to make eye contact with him, smiling as I turned to face him, "good afternoon. How are you this afternoon?" The officer appeared relaxed and confident. I expected him to be a bit annoyed at having been sent for. He didn't show it, if he was.

I proceeded to ask Officer Smith a series of questions about where his cruiser was at the point when he first observed my vehicle (A red two door sedan with a white vinyl top), and where my vehicle was at the same point in time. His answer as to his own location was correct. He was entering the freeway from the on-ramp. He said my vehicle was in the number one (inside) lane (there were four lanes in each direction in that area of the freeway). He said my car was about four or five car lengths ahead.

When I asked him about the placement and the number of the other vehicles around me and between his cruiser and my car, he began to lose his cool demeanor. He was unable to state clearly how many other vehicles were around my car and between his vehicle and mine. He got a little rattled and then, a little embarrassed, which produced the result I was seeking. He became annoyed and started to lose his concentration.

I went through a long series of questions about traffic conditions; weather conditions, the condition of the roadway, where he had come from when he was getting on the freeway, and on and on. The Judge was getting impatient. She had created for herself, a situation that was going to result in a long day, and was not happy about it. When I paused for a look at my notes (for effect), she asked, "Are you finished with your questions?" "No, your honor, thank you, I have some more questions. I'll try to be brief." "Yes, you do that ", she snipped. "Yes Ma'am, your Honor, thank you:, I said flashing her my best "thanks for you help" smile, as I spoke and rearranged my notes. I was getting what I wanted from her, too. She was extremely distracted, edgy and un-focused. The prosecutor seemed not the least bit interested. That was fine with me.

Another smile and nod of my head to Officer Smith, and I asked him about his speedometer calibration dates, certifications and such. He could not tell me when the calibrations had been made; couldn't recall "off the top of my head", he said. He did not have any kind of documentation with him attesting to the fact that the speedometer had *ever* been calibrated. At that moment, I was in danger of making the mistake of laughing out loud - or at least cracking a big grin. With great difficulty, I suppressed the urge to chuckle and, instead, announced to the Judge, my motion to dismiss, on the grounds that there was no evidence, or even testimony, before the court attesting to the fact that the speedometer was ever calibrated as required by law.

Poor Madam Judge, at that point she lost it. I don't think she even listened to my words beyond the point of announcing my motion to dismiss."Your motion is denied", she loudly snapped at me. "Now I am sick of all this endless chatter from you. Do you understand? I want this business concluded here", she went on. I looked at her about the same way everyone in the courtroom did . . . as if to ask if she was going to be okay. She was glaring at me and rapidly making little nods of her head. "Yes Ma'am, I'll try to get finished here, your Honor, and, please Ma'am, note for the record, my exception to your dismissal of my motion, I said.

Next, I reached into the brown paper bag and removed a coke can and two tissues. The tissues were deformed from having been wrapped around the coke can when it was cold and wet. Everyone was watching intently as I removed the items. I held the coke can up in my outstretched hand and said, "Do you recognize this, Officer Smith?" "It's a coke can", he said, clearly puzzled as everyone in the room seemed to be. "No, Officer Smith, it's *not* a coke can", I said, pausing to add effect to my words. "It's *the* coke can, Officer Smith, the one I had in my car the day you stopped me; the day you thought it was a *beer* can. It's the can you saw me take a drink from after I passed the car that was driving in front of me at forty-five miles an hour in the number two lane."

Then I picked up the two tissues, holding them up for all to see. "You recognize these, don't you, Officer Smith? These are the tissues that were wrapped around this cold, wet can, you know, the same tissues that had fallen away from the can as it sat in my console cup holder. You remember, don't you? You came up alongside my car on the passenger side and looked into my car through the power window I had already rolled down for you as you approached my car. You had already begun to speak, remember? You said, 'I stopped you because you were drin . . . uhh . . . driving too fast', you said . . . as you noticed that the can I had been drinking from was this *coke* can . . . and not a *beer* can..."

A sound came from the Bench; from the judge. I can't describe the sound, other than to say I sounded something like a *buzzer*. The sound got everyone's attention. The Judge glared icily at me, clearly struggling to maintain her composure, what little there was left. There was a long pause. I weighed the situation and felt I had gotten all I could out of my cross-examination of the Officer. I had plenty of grounds for appeal "Are you finished?" the Judge snarled. I was sure this Judge was going to find me guilty; that she had decided earlier in the day, even before the trial, perhaps even before she set eyes on me. "Yes, your Honor, I'm finished", I said.

The Judge shifted around a bit in her chair, looked straight at me and said, "Good! Now then . . . I am going to find you guilty . . ." "Excuse me, your Honor", I blurted out with some elevated volume. "Are you saying I don't even get an opportunity to testify? And you're going to find me guilty without my being able to testify in my own defense?"

Concentration is so important! Concentration! I have never seen anyone lose his or her concentration as much as that Judge did. I almost felt sorry for her. The looks on the faces around the courtroom (and their numbers, I realized, had grown since this trial had started) can only be described as incredulous.

"You said you were finished", she said in almost a whine. "You asked me if I was finished with my cross examination of Officer Smith, and I said I was", I replied. "But I never heard of a defendant not being allowed to testify in his own behalf", I went on, shaking my head in disbelief. Could I have ever been given a stronger lock on winning an appeal than this, I wondered? As I reflected on this extraordinary turn of events, the Judge interrupted my thoughts. "Well", she said in a voice that revealed she was clearly shaken (no doubt thinking about the humiliation of being reversed down the line), "If you want to testify, then by all means do so."

"Well I don't know how much good it will do me to testify, since you have already decided to find me guilty, but yes, I will testify, indeed. And please note my exception for the record to your conduct of this trial, you Honor", I added.

I then recited my testimony. It was all written in my script and well rehearsed. It didn't sound as though I was reading it, because I wasn't. I had my testimony memorized. I had even memorized responses to some anticipated questions I would get from the prosecutor on his cross examination. This was all unnecessary. There was no cross-examination. The judge looked like she wasn't listening to a word I was saying. But anyone could see the wheels turning in her head as I went on with my testimony. When I finished, she didn't even glance my way. She looked over at the prosecutor. He didn't even wait for her to ask. "I have nothing further, you Honor", he said.

The judge had regained some composure while I testified. She cleared her throat, avoided eye contact with me, instead, directing her glare at Officer Smith. "Officer Smith", she began, "this is a perfect example of poor performance! Because you chose to perform so poorly, I have no choice but to dismiss the case against this defendant. Not only did you make a mess of this case with the improper citation, but also then you showed up in this court without the proper documentation of your calibrations or not even knowing when they were done. I hope, if you ever appear in my court again, Officer Smith, you will come prepared! This case is dismissed. The defendant may go."

Victory! How sweet it is. It had been a long day, but had ended well. I was glad to win, but not especially happy about the way it all came together; or should I say all came apart? It never ceases to amaze me how important it is to maintain one's concentration on the task at hand, whatever it might be. And if Officer Smith had recognized that at the beginning, he could have saved himself and all of us the inconvenience.

I didn't feel sorry for the Officer, even though the judge made him the fall guy for her own gross errors. *I really had been drinking a coke that day.* I had been in the number two lane, driving between fifty-five and sixty miles per hour. The car ahead of me was tooling along at the breath-taking speed of a bit less than forty-five.

The number one lane was clear, so I signaled a lane change, passed the other car, signaled again after I picked him up in my rear view mirror and changed back into the number two lane. At that point, I took a swallow of the coke and set it back into the holder. I had seen the trooper entering the freeway when I changed lanes the second time.

I probably *was* speeding to the tune of about fifty-seven or fifty-eight miles per hour. Seventy-two miles per hour was a much-used number by the troopers. I heard it often in courts as I listened to other cases. That officer made an error for whatever reason, he just wasn't going to admit it and go on about his business. His mistake.

Once, a long time ago, I had a night job as a machine mechanic at a bubble gum factory in New York where all of the machine operators were women. The operators fed long ropes of bubble gum into the machines that shaped, cut and wrapped the small pieces of bubble gum. The machines frequently jammed when the sticky build up of gum would cause the gum ropes to stick. The operators had a tool to scrape out the rope track and clear jams. If they followed procedure, they stopped the machine and cleared the jam. Most did not follow procedure and would try to clear jams with the machine still running. On average, about three to four times a month an operator would have a finger sliced off and wrapped in a bubble gum wrapper. I learned a lot about concentration on that job.

Here is yet another example of the power of concentration. Football is a great and popular sport in America. It is also a great laboratory for developing boys and young men into leaders. Concentration is one of the most important lessons to be learned in the sport of football. As one who played the game as a boy and coached the game as a man, for twelve years, I can attest to the absolute importance of concentration.

Many years ago, when I was coaching the Westbury Steers Junior Varsity team in the Football United National League in Houston, Texas, we had a game with our arch-rival West University Shamrocks. It was in the final moments of the game . . . Westbury 13, West University 7. Westbury had the lead and had the ball on our own 2 yard line . . . fourth down, with 39 seconds left in the game, and we did not have a punter.

I called time out and brought my Tailback (we ran a single wing offense) over to the sideline. "Bobby", I said, "Call a 46 (a sweep right) in the huddle. Take the snap and kneel down in the end zone." Bobby looked at me as if I was crazy. "Bobby", I said, "Don't think about it. Just do it. Trust me", I said.

The team huddled up. Bobby called the play, took the snap and knelt down in the end zone, as I had instructed him to do. I was focused on watching the other side of the field. I watched as the Shamrocks celebrated the fact that they had "scored" a Safety against us . . . two points . . . Westbury 13, West University 9. I continued watching seeing the celebration on the other side of the field fade away as they all realized what had just happened to them.

When you give up a Safety, you get a free kick. We had an excellent kick-off kicker. We made our free kick and the game ended at the other end of the field on the Shamrocks' thirteen yard line. Westbury 13, West University 9.

Concentration won . . . as it always does.

Now I will relate the first part of what I will call the Valley Radar Caper. I mentioned the judge-pro-tem from this bizarre case earlier. Driving, one day, through the San Fernando Valley along the Ventura Freeway, I was stopped by a highway patrolman and given a citation for exceeding the maximum speed - you guessed it, seventy-two miles per hour. (You may be wondering about the phrase "exceeding the maximum speed".

The reason I use that phrase is because that is the exact phrase that appears on the citation; not just the word "speeding". That's because, in California, where those cases I've written about has two speed laws, or at least did then. The "Maximum Speed law" was violated if you exceeded the speed posted on signs that stated "Maximum Speed XX". The "Basic Speed law" was applied on roads that had signs stating: "Speed Limit XX"). There are more complications involved in the Basic Speed law; things like the eighty-five percentile studies and such that I won't get into here. But whatever State I am in, I will make it an absolutely top priority to learn all I can about the traffic laws.

In the Valley Radar Caper, I went to court and was ready for trial. The officer was in court; I had my game plan all set as usual, and was confident I would win, as I always am. Then, several unusual circumstances were revealed. First, The Judge was not a Judge, but a *Judge-Pro-Tem*, which is a Lawyer who is sort of like a Non-Certificated substitute Teacher. He's a Lawyer that some panel has decided has enough expertise to act in the capacity of a Judge in Certain kinds of cases. Then, Second, we learned that the Prosecutor was also a *Prosecutor-Pro-Tem*. I am not certain, but I don't believe there were any *Defendant-Pro-Tems* in the court that day.

My case was called and the Prosecutor-Pro-Tem put the officer through his paces pretty well. On Cross examination, I followed my typical plan, asking the officer many questions about details of lanes, numbers and locations of vehicles and all of that. When I got to the point where I asked the officer about the speedometer calibrations and requested that he show the Court the certifications . . . as expected, the officer did not have the certification documents.

As usual, I moved for dismissal on the grounds that there was no evidence before the Court, beyond hearsay, to confirm that the speedometer had ever been calibrated, as required by law. At that point, the Judge-Pro-Tem asked the officer where the documentation was. The officer said the documents were back at his station in the West Valley. We were in Van Nuys, many miles away, in the East Valley. The Judge-Pro-Tem who, incidentally, had held my case to last on the docket because I was going to trial instead of pleading guilty, said, "very well, we will recess while you go back to the station and retrieve those documents. We will reconvene at one o'clock." At the time he said that, it was about eleven fifteen in the morning. I protested, as you might imagine and got nothing but an opportunity to emphatically ask the Judge-Pro-Tem to note my exception for the record, which brought an audible snicker from the guy.

Well, this development did not sit well with the Prosecutor-Pro-Tem either, who probably had other plans for the afternoon, like maybe a round of golf. I know it to be true that it did not sit well with him, because when the Judge-Pro-Tem announced we would reconvene at one o'clock, I clearly heard the Prosecutor-Pro-Tem say, "Oh, Bullshit!

I'm not coming back here at one o'clock." He did not say the words loud enough for the Judge-Pro-Tem to hear them. He was talking to an associate at the Prosecutors' table. But, though probably not intentionally, he said the words loud enough for me to hear them.

I was thinking I had caught a break. We would reconvene, I reasoned, and the Prosecutor-Pro-Tem would not show up. The Judge-Pro-Tem would have to dismiss. I was in for a major surprise; a shock I couldn't believe. When Court was again called to order, with the officer back from his trip to the station, documents in hand, the Judge-Pro-Tem asked where the Prosecutor was. No one seemed to know. I spoke up. "Your Honor", I said, "When you announced the recess, the Prosecutor said, 'Oh Bullshit, I'm not coming back here at one o'clock." There was scattered laughter from the few people in court, including the Judge-Pro-Tem. "Oh well", he said. "I can handle the Prosecution. It's no big deal." I launched myself from my chair at the Defense Table and objected. I informed the Judge-Pro-Tem that I was moving for dismissal and that I had a Constitutional right to a trial by an impartial Judge. He could not function as the Prosecutor and be impartial, I declared.

He responded that yes, he certainly could and that was how we were going to do it. "Oh, you think so? We'll see about that you Son of a Bitch", were the words bubbling up in my mind, as I visualized stepping forward, yanking him off the Bench and dumping him on the floor . . . but my Guardian Angel took control and stopped me.

Once again, I stated my exception for the record and emphatically added that I would march right down to the Clerk's Office after this mock trial and file my appeal immediately.

Does it sound like I lost my concentration? Sure . . . I was stupefied! I lost every trace of my concentration. As I expected, the Judge-Pro-Tem found me guilty and, true to my word, I went directly to the Clerk's Office and filed my appeal. You will read about the startling outcome of my appeal in Chapter twelve.

CHAPTER TEN

Witnesses' Testimony

I prepare and rehearse mine….

Having a witness to appear in court and testify on my behalf, supporting my version of the facts related to the case is a good thing, isn't it? The simple, short answer is *"maybe"*. The key is how well the witness performs, and how credible the witness appears to the Court. The problem with this issue is that I can't be certain how well the witness will do in court. No amount of preparation and practice will guarantee the witness' convincing performance in the actual trial setting.

In my experience, over many years, I have seldom had the luxury, or is it the liability (?) of having a witness appear on my behalf. That is due to two things: First, my visits to Traffic Court have always been in connection with an alleged moving violation or an alleged mechanical defect in my vehicle. I have never been cited for, or been a defendant in a case involving liability, such as property damage or bodily injury. Second, I have some misgivings about the value of the testimony of a witness in most traffic cases that do not involve property damage or bodily injury.

Let's consider a hypothetical case in which I was cited for doing 78 miles per hour on a 65 mile per hour maximum speed freeway. It is essentially the traffic officer's testimony against mine. If I had a passenger or passengers in my vehicle when I was cited, she or they could testify to certain facts if I called her or them as witnesses. The problem, as I see it, is that there is a murky area that may creep into the mix. Personal observations and experiences in court have led me to be wary of bringing a witness into court to help me win by overpowering the officer's testimony.

It's a bit of overkill that, from what I have seen and heard in courts, tends to make an "underdog" of the officer. God, forbid! If there is going to be an underdog in the courtroom, I want him to be me. Be it a trial before a Judge, or a jury trial, I am convinced that a perceived "underdog" develops an edge over his or her opponent. It's an almost universal, but certainly American, trait to back the underdog. People of all stripes just seem to want to help an "underdog". Therefore, I don't easily accept the idea of bringing a witness to court with me.

If, however, there were some extraordinary circumstances that came into play during the traffic stop, I might become convinced of the logic and wisdom of bringing a witness to court. Suppose, for example, the officer was having a particularly bad day, since his wife had just informed him she was leaving him for the guy who leans the pool. Let's say he storms up to my driver's side window, which I have already politely rolled down to accommodate our meeting, and he screams at me to get my "bleep, bleep butt out of the car". Then, when I obey his order and get out, he launches into a profanity laced tirade in which he calls into question my family lineage and informs me that I am an ignorant piece of a certain foul waste material. Finally, he writes the citation accusing me of speeding and tells me to get my sorry carcass out of his sight. Now let's say that, through all of this, my passenger, or three passengers have been sitting in my car, stunned by the officer's astonishing performance. In such a case, yes, I would bring all of the witnesses I could to court with me.

However, I would not bring those witnesses to testify to my speed. What I would want them to testify to is the out of control, over the edge conduct of the officer, and my own rational, sane handling of the situation. My intent would be to have the witnesses lend credibility to my own testimony, in which I would relate that the officer appeared and acted in a manner that suggested he was clearly in a troubled state of mind and that he had erred in everything he did in connection with that particular traffic stop. I do not want anyone to fantasize too much about the hypothetical tale I just related. Those things do not happen often enough, in my opinion, to make a blip on any radar screen. Cops are not crazy or stupid. They are trained individuals who basically know what they are doing. But they are still human beings who sometimes make mistakes. Just do not hold your breath until you see the scenario like the one described above.

The thing I consider pertinent and important is that it would take some highly unusual circumstances at the time of the citation to influence me to bring a witness to court for something like a speeding ticket.

When it comes to a citation for a violation that also involves property damage or bodily injury, for which I stood accused, I would certainly want to have the support of a credible witness or witnesses. The same would hold true if I were cited for an "under the influence" violation. If possible, I would want to have testimony from a believable witness or two who could attest to the fact that I was not impaired. In any case where I found myself cited for a violation that involved Property damage or bodily injury . . . or even more importantly, an under the influence case, I would definitely not represent myself in court. The are lines we should never cross.

 In any trial where I decided to bring witnesses to testify on my behalf, I would do so only after having thoroughly prepared the witness or witnesses. The preparation would include a complete review of all of the facts as I saw them, all of the questions I would plan to ask the witnesses, the likely cross-examination challenges I believed the Prosecutor would make to the witnesses testimony, and the answers I would want the witnesses to use to those challenges.

Under no circumstances, ever, would I ask a witness to lie or bend the truth in any way. That would be wrong and foolhardy. I would, however, work very hard with the witness to prepare and rehearse – yes, rehearse –him or her on the desirable testimony and answers to likely cross-examination challenges.

If the prospective witness was not willing to work with me on the preparation and rehearsal session, I would not bring the witness to court, period; end of story. A poor supporting witness is like a witness for the other side, devastating. Preparation is paramount.

I Respect Theirs . . .

In the same manner as I would prepare my own witnesses and rehearse them until I was confident they would be an asset to my side, I would prepare myself and rehearse my plan to attack and discredit any witness appearing for the other side, as carefully and deceptively as possible. Here I may be a t some disadvantage. I may not know who will appear as a witness against me for the other side. In all probability, I will not know for certain, even if there will be any witnesses for the other side and against me. It is not as hopeless as it might seem.

First. I will assume there is an individual who will appear against me. I will analyze the circumstances of the case, and consider the fact that the other side will use the witness to establish certain points. I consider "use" the operative word here. Yes, witnesses are tools to be used in a trial against the opposition, to convince the court or the jury of something that will weigh heavily against the opposition. Once I had determined a generic list of prospective points related to the facts of the case that the other side may wish to hammer home to the court, I would then plan my Cross examination of such a witness.

I would prepare a script of questions to ask the witness on Cross. The questions would be designed to accomplish my goal of showing the witness to be unbelievable. In order to do that, I may carefully ask some questions that may rattle the witness; make him or her nervous enough to make contradictory statements. In no way will I treat the witness disrespectfully; nor will I take an antagonistic approach toward the witness. I will actually try to win over the witness, get him comfortable and relaxed. Then in the most polite way I can, I will ask a question, or series of disarming questions of the witness, designed to cause the witness to contradict himself and lose credibility.

There is a line I will never cross when questioning a witness on cross. It is a very difficult line to distinguish, different in each situation. It is the line that, if I cross it, turns the tide against me. Crossing that line will probably cause the witness to become completely rattled, perhaps even to the point of tears. At the same time, the jury will view me as a bully, a predator, taking advantage of a poor nervous witness to mask the truth of my own guilt. Because the line I speak of is so difficult to see in time not to cross it, I pay extremely close attention to how the witness is reacting to the questions I am asking and to the word selection, tone and timber of voice used by the witness. If I am alert and careful, even to the point of being protective of the witness's sensibilities and feelings, at some point, just before the line, I will see, but not cross it.

Then, using all the acting ability I can muster, I will make some mild statement concerning the errors or inaccuracy of the witness's testimony, mixed in with my offer of thanks to the witness for his or her cooperation. The tone of my voice and inflection in my words; without any condescension, will communicate to the Jury the message I want them to "hear" without actually having to say the words . . . that, even though the witness has made statements about me or the circumstances of the case which are actually not true, I do not believe he or she was intentionally trying to harm me and I bear no ill will toward the witness.

There are facial expressions that go with the process. You know them and use them on certain occasions. When your child does something wrong and you have to administer some form of discipline, there is that look; that sad facial expression you show the child as you softly speak the message of how disappointed you are, but know he didn't mean to hurt you by his disobedient behavior, and how sure you are he will try to never disappoint you again. You get the idea.

If I have prepared well and chosen carefully the questions I put to the witness, asked those questions respectfully, and effectively communicated to the Jury, without ever actually coming out saying so, that the witness's statements are not true, I will erase the credibility of the testimony at least enough to raise doubts about the accuracy of the statements.

As important as I believe it is to treat the Officer who cited me, the Prosecutor and the Judge respectfully, treating the witness I am cross-examining respectfully is even more important. Even a hostile or surly witness must be handled with the utmost respect; Perhaps even more so than a polite witness. In fact, I would rather cross-examine a witness with bad manners and a harsh or crude demeanor because of the opportunities such a witness creates for me to undermine his or her believability.

An important point to remember is that the truth is always the most powerful weapon to use in any battle of words or wits. The truth is, though, there are many ways to use the weapon of the truth and not everyone knows that. To illustrate that concept, let me give this example: We live in a world where we are constantly bombarded with "STATISTICS". Virtually every segment of our society uses statistics at one turn or another to illustrate some important point or convince someone of the value, danger, joy, sadness, alarm, etc. of this or that set of statistics.

In fact, you and I can each make a case, absolutely contrary to each other's case, using only the "Truth" of the same statistics. LET ME SHOW YOU HOW. Say that Ajax Computer Corporation releases a set of statistics showing that the company's production of desktop PC's amounted to total units of three million in 1990, with increases each year through 1998 of three more million per year. By constructing a horizontal line graph one way, showing the years 1990 through 1998 along the bottom of the graph, and production in increments of 3MM units along the left side, then drawing in the line representing the annual unit production, I could Caption the Graph "Desktop PC Production Climbs Gradually".

In Contrast, using the identical numbers – the same "Truth" – and constructing a Graph with a different layout, you could title your Graph "Desktop PC Production Soars". How? Simply by arranging your graph in a vertical layout, with the years starting with 1990, and ending 1998, along the bottom. Production levels listed on the right in 3MM increments. The production would extend from the bottom left upward to the top right beginning with 3MM at left and continuing upward to 27MM, the line would have the appearance of a meteoric rise.

The point of all this is to illustrate that I go to Traffic court to win. And I win by being smarter, or more determined, or maybe just luckier than my opponent is. However I manage it, I have to cause my opponent to make a mistake that costs him the game. I won't go into court and lie. But if I can devise a way to present my version of the truth in a way that is different than my opponent's way, and the Jury likes my way better, you bet I'm going to use that tool. The most likely scenario for my using the tool of presenting truth in a different way will be to neutralize a witness against me, or maybe even to get him to bolster my case by agreeing with me.

How to deal with witnesses, theirs or mine, is very tricky. I do not believe I will ever feel as comfortable dealing with a witness as I do dealing with the officer, the prosecutor, or the judge. As with most everything else in traffic court, though, the key to successfully using or challenging witnesses is advance preparation.

CHAPTER ELEVEN

Defendant's Testimony

I plan, prepare and rehearse . . .

I have seen more people than I could count go into traffic court to try their case without a shred of planning or preparation. Usually, they not only end up paying fines and penalty assessments and the like, but look like fools doing it. If I lose a case in traffic court, I guarantee I will not make a fool of myself in the process. What's more, if I lose, I will probably receive a lesser fine than I would have, had I walked into court and just paid up, or did something even more foolish, like pleading "guilty with an explanation". The latter is what I consider a "Masochist Plea".

What makes me think, you might ask, I would receive a lesser fine if I try my case and lose? It's simple. It's about how I conduct myself in court. I show respect for the process, treat my adversaries with respect and show up prepared, with a clear intention of winning. People like winners. People, cops, judges and prosecutors included, respect people who show respect for the system and have the courage of their convictions, stand for what they believe in. Oh, I know there are lots of folks who will say that's corny or that it's bunk. I'm here to tell you they are wrong. They are the folks who go in and enter that slick plea of "guilty with an explanation". Sure, on rare occasions a benevolent judge will go easy on them. That happens about as often as a lunar eclipse. What's more important to me is that doesn't happen as a result of the judge or prosecutor having any respect for the person either. It's more like the judge looking at the person and thinking "what a pathetic case. I'll go easy on this sad sack; only take a case and a half of beans off his table, instead of two cases". Okay, maybe I'm being unkind, but I simply do not believe in presenting myself as a sniveler.

As the Defendant in my traffic court case, I like to start off by seeing myself in a positive light. Do not misunderstand when I say I look upon the approaching event during the preparatory stages with great and positive anticipation. That traffic court trial is going to be the big show, the main event. Best of all, I am going to have the starring role. I am the center of the whole program. And, above all else, I will have the privilege of exercising my rights. Most people in the world never have such power to act! If that sounds corny to anyone, I'd like to take that person on a tour of some of the places I've seen in this world, including some western European countries.

Fine! I've said my piece. It's time to get on with the good stuff. As the star of the show, the defendant's testimony, my testimony, is the stuff of the highlight reel.

By the time I come to the trial, I have done most of my planning and preparation. I have virtually completed my script and rehearsed it several times. The script will have open slots at several points to insert additional comments and statements in response to, or to refute statements or claims made by the officer and/or any witnesses the prosecutor has put on. In some instances, I may want to add to my testimony because of a comment made by the judge during the officer's testimony or my cross-examination of him or any other prosecution witness who may have testified.

When my turn to testify comes, I will have already inserted any additional statements or comments I want to add. I will also have made notes during the prosecution's case that will help me to anticipate, and be prepared to respond to, specific points the prosecutor may challenge in his cross-examination of me. Have I made the picture clear? Is there any doubt that I am prepared, rehearsed and raring to go by that point?

All through the trial prior to my own testimony, I will have made certain that all of the parties have seen and noted that I have made copious notes. Why? What's the difference? The difference is that I begin right away to establish that I am here on a mission, that I am not some whiner who just set the case for trial hoping the officer would not show up and the case would be dismissed. Oh, I'll certainly welcome that outcome if it presents itself. But the truth is, I want the officer to be in court. I want to grill him, rattle him, un-nerve him and cause him to lose his concentration . . . cause him to lose . . . but all in a very gentlemanly manner, of course.

There is yet another reason for the copious note taking . . . and it really doesn't matter what I write, or weather I even use any of it. The reason is simply that it works in my favor as a very subtle psychological tool. Be it a judge or a jury, but more so with a jury, the note taking sends a message that I am confident and sure of my own innocence of the offense I was cited for. The note taking very subtly reinforces my believability factor.

Every time I jot something down, someone in that jury, perhaps several of the jurors, will entertain a thought . . . something along the lines of "Uh-Oh, he's caught him on something again". I know this to be true, because I have actually had a juror tell me on two separate occasions that they noticed that . . ."every time I caught him in a lie or a mistake, I made a note of it". The note taking helps me, or doesn't help me. I'll go with it helps.

Whether it's a jury or a judge hearing the case I have, by then, made a positive impression. Every person in the courtroom knows that I mean business; that I am here to win. They can feel my innocence from the determination I've shown from the start. This is not some guy trying to beat a ticket. He's trying to prove he is innocent. I want to be sure that I've done that. It lends credence to me (even in the mind of the guy in the third row who may, for some reason, or no reason at, wants me to lose) and gives weight to my testimony. Early in my testimony, I will make certain to work in a statement emphasizing that I have a clean driving record and am a responsible, conscientious driver. Remember, a citation ends up on my driving record, only if it results in a conviction.

By then, the judge and jury are being drawn into the *perception* that I must be innocent of the charge that the officer must have erred . . . or lied. Everyone knows in their own mind about *quotas* . . . I know this to be a reasonable assumption, because jurors have commented to me more than once that they "knew" I had to be innocent because I was so persistent, or because I gave so many details, etc.. The point, as one juror once told me, was why would I have gone to all the trouble of the trial and all, if I were guilty? What his comment taught me was that people tend to *receive* you as they *perceive* you.

Even if the jurors come into the courtroom with the preconceived bias that the defendant is probably guilty – why would the cop give him a ticket for nothing? Once the trial gets underway and I present myself in such a positive way, while at the same time showing absolute respect for the system and the opponents, such preconceived biases tend to evaporate rather quickly. If I look like a winner, act like a winner and talk like a winner, I must **be** a winner.

As I say so often, people want to be on the side of a winner. Perhaps more importantly, people want to make a winner of someone they perceive as deserving to be a winner. Someone seen as an underdog is often also perceived as deserving to be a winner. Helping that person to actually be a winner gives many of those people great satisfaction from knowing they helped put him over the top. Look at how people react to stars of the movies or sports. Those stars have never really done anything for the people who revere them. What happens is that many people feel great vicarious pleasure from the notion that they are somehow responsible in part for the star's success because they support the stars and help them reach the heights.

Sound too heavy? Yes, I admit it does. But I believe millions of people behave in just that way. I could be wrong. But I don't think so.

CHAPTER TWELVE

Appeals

It Ain't Over "Til The Fat Cats Sing

We all have guideposts in our lives; concepts, ideals, principals we live by. One of the most powerful, most energizing and most sustaining guidepost I follow (I think of my guidepost as "Life-Links", principals that are components of my personal code of living) is this: Never, Never, Never, Ever give up – Persevere".

In pioneer days, those people who gave up the trials and hardships they faced along the trail in search of their dreams, frequently died. Not only did they not fulfill their dream; they also did not fulfill their full potential. Yes, it is easy for me, who never had to endure the terrible hardships faced by the Pioneers, to say those words. But I do not make that assessment in the spirit of ridicule. Rather, I view it from the perspective of sadness and loss . . . and as a means to keep me focused on what is really important and valuable in life. Because the Pioneers, and others who followed them into the wilderness areas as this Nation grew, struggled and persevered against so many obstacles and dangers, we do not have to endure many of the deprivations that were part of their everyday lives.

We face trials and obstacles today that come in **disguise**. The freedoms and treasures won for us by our courageous forebears are ever more rapidly falling into **danger**. We are gradually losing many of our liberties, bit by bit. More and more of our people abuse those precious liberties, or take for granted our freedom. More and more others of our people react to abuses and neglect with calls for the abolition of rights. *These are dangerous times.* The danger lies in the apathy of so many of our friends and neighbors.

One of the most important attributes of freedom, perhaps the *most* important of all, is the widely *ignored* universal truth that freedom is *not free.* Free people must bear a proportional burden of responsibility for the protection and preservation of their freedom, if they are to remain free people.

I have heard people tell me I take these traffic court matters too seriously; that I make them out to be more important than they are. I do not. Others who came before me purchased for me any and every freedom or right I enjoy today, at great human cost. I *respect* that. One of the ways I respect that fact is in my commitment to keeping the system strong. The way to keep the system strong is to use it, as it was created to be used.

If I lose my case in traffic court, something happened to derail my plan. Throughout the trial, I make notes on all that is happening. The purpose of the note taking is to keep focused on the plan and the task at hand, which is: winning my case. It bears repeating that I am in traffic court because I *made an error.* I do not want to be treated unfairly as a result of my error. As strong as my belief in the American system is, I believe that the traffic courts of this land can barely be considered to be a part of the judicial system. A mere thread on the fringe, in my view, attaches them to the real judicial system. Traffic courts, based on what I have observed, experienced and studied for many years, are not about justice and truth. Nor are they about promoting more safety on the road. Traffic courts are about revenue. Furthermore, too much of the revenue generated in the traffic court process, in my opinion, goes to bureaucrats and other non-productive hangers-on who contribute nothing toward justice or safety.

Remember, my potential for victory does not, necessarily, end in traffic court. I have the right to appeal any traffic court decision if the court has failed to comply with the rules of law. One of the fundamental reasons I do so much advance research and preparation before my trial is to uncover points of law that are **frequently ignored** in traffic courts. I have observed for many decades a traffic court mindset and what I perceive to be an ingrained, almost institutional, attitude of not having to be bothered with the **small details** of the law. But, when crunch time comes . . . there are no small details. Whomever coined the phrase "The Devil is in the details" knew what he or she was talking about.

As an example, I have never seen or heard of any judge asking an officer in a radar case if he had, with him in court, documentary proof – evidence that his radar unit was inspected and calibrated, as required by law. But, conversely, I have on numerous occasions seen judges brush the issue aside, when raised by a defendant, and actually find that defendant guilty, despite the lack of evidence that the radar unit was legal. Such egregious behavior by a judge would most definitely be a point of law upon which I would base an appeal, were I the defendant in such a case. Judges, too, must abide by the law and actions have consequences, even for judges.

Any time I have the option to file an appeal (where I do have a reasonable point of law basis to make an appeal) I will definitely file the appeal. My rational is simple. I want to be treated right by the court. If the court ignores a point of law for whatever reason to get a conviction, I will vigorously seek redress. As a matter of fact, aside from the aspect of righting a wrong and saving money, there is a special sweetness that goes with winning on appeal. No judge wants to be reversed. But in the day to day routine of traffic court, sometimes judges get lazy or careless – or pompous. That is why I never fail to speak out, loud and clear, during the trial and ask the judge to "Please note my objection (or my exception) for the record", anytime he denies a motion or takes any action I consider to be contrary to my rights under the law.

When I make that statement, it makes the judge aware that I know I have rights in his court . . . and will likely seek redress. The effect, usually, is that the judge is more careful about not stepping on my rights, and more likely to require the prosecutor and the officer to actually prove their case.

I will revisit the Valley Radar Caper case now and present the details of the outcome of the Appeal I filed. I was furious over the way the judge-pro-tem conducted the trial. It was, and still is in my mind, an outright mockery of the justice system. That a so-called officer of the court would dare, so blatantly, to deny anyone the constitutional right to a fair and impartial trial seemed inconceivable. Yet, I believed then, as I do today, that was precisely what had occurred.

I have never been a member of the American Civil liberties Union. I have, in fact, despised many of the stands they have taken through the years, particularly on religion related issues (I still send Christmas Card Blessings to the ACLU every year . . . disguised in a standard business envelope, to ensure it gets opened, wishing God's Christmas Blessings on them). But on this occasion, I decided to call them and see what they had to say.

I called the Los Angeles office of the ACLU and spoke to one of their lawyers. I asked him if they would be interested in hearing about a case where the judge had decided to be the prosecutor, as well as the judge. Yes, indeed they would be interested, I was told, and gave the lawyer the particulars of the case over the phone.

Two days after I spoke to the ACLU Lawyer, he called me with some incredibly bad news. My appeal was dead meat, in so many words, the lawyer told me. He explained that the

California Supreme Court, in a decision issued in the early 1980's, ruled that a judge could, indeed, act as prosecutor and judge in **infraction** cases. The purported justification for the decision was that the defendant's liberty and property are not at risk in an infraction case, or some words to that effect.

I hate to lose . . . EVER. But we all must lose some of the time. Losing this particular case, though, made me physically sick to my stomach. As I see it, I lost a traffic case. Okay, I can deal with that. But in the course of losing that particular case I discovered that I, and all of the people of California, had already lost a whole lot more. The activist "Rose Bird" California Supreme Court had **taken from us** the right to a fair and impartial trial in infraction cases. I consider that to be a great Shame and a Disgrace. I doubt that the California Supreme Court's decision could withstand a challenge in the United States Supreme Court, though I don't believe such a challenge has ever been mounted. With public apathy being what it is in our times, it's likely such a challenge will never be made.

Make no mistake, though, about the bogus basis for this rogue Court's decision. A defendant's liberty **and** property most certainly **are** at risk in an infraction case. If found Guilty, the defendant's likely penalty will be a fine and fees . . . dollars, which are the **Property** of the Defendant. If the fine is not paid then, at some point, the Defendant will be arrested and **placed in Jail.** Thus, the defendant's **Property as well as his Liberty are supremely at risk.**

My position is simple and straightforward. If we as a people allow any political body to strip away our lesser rights, it is only a question of time until we lose enough of our freedom as to be no longer free.

A Special Note: I originally wrote the paragraph above in early 2000. As I write this paragraph for the Revised Edition now, in March 2012, and reflect on the enormous number of additional freedoms and rights that have been abridged or stolen from us over the years since 2000, by renegade politicians, Judges, bureaucrats and even "Czars", I can barely rise above the sadness I feel at the state of our country. I pray that Americans will do all it takes to restore all of our lost rights and freedoms. Traffic Courts are a good place to start.

CHAPTER THIRTEEN

A Funny Thing Happened . . .
. . . On The Way To Press

As I prepared the manuscript for this book to go to press, I found some parts of the content made me a little edgy. The reason was that some passages sounded like instructions or lessons. I became concerned because I had heard in the previous couple of years or so, a flurry of stories in the media about individuals, writers and others, being accused of the so-called charge of "Unauthorized Practice of Law".

I am not a lawyer. In fact, I am tempted to add the words "thank God" to that declaration. I have no desire or plan to become a lawyer. Should the day ever come when I decide that I want to practice law, I will go back to law school, earn the degree, take the Bar exam, and get a law license. Believe me when I tell you that is not a likely scenario.

There was a period in time, years ago when I was a licensed Private Investigator, that I entertained the idea of running for the State Legislature and going back to law school and getting my law degree.

The rationale for that was that State Legislators (at least, at that time) got unlimited continuances for their cases in court. That, I reasoned, was something that surely must add considerable weight to such a lawyer's win percentage. However, I spent a good deal of time in and around courtrooms during that period and observed firsthand the ins and outs of court routine . . . the plea bargains and all of the other goings on that I saw as sordid and tawdry and soon concluded that it was a process that I did not want to be a part of.

Far less likely than my becoming a lawyer, not likely at all in fact, is the prospect that I would attempt to engage in the practice of law without a license.

Because I felt uncomfortable with some of the passages in the book, I opted to go back and do a number of re-writes, to remove the passages that I felt may have sounded more instructional than anecdotal and replace them. During the re-writing period, two interesting traffic court situations arose. Actually one of the two matters was a traffic ticket not actually traffic **Court** related. The two cases were interesting enough, I believed, to be included in these pages.

In September, 1997, I was driving to the post office in mid-afternoon on a residential street, slower than the posted 30 mile per hour posted speed. I was in no hurry.

As I proceeded southbound on the street, a divided boulevard with a wide center esplanade and two traffic lanes in each direction, there was a school bus about one and a half blocks ahead, moving in the same direction. The school bus was in the right hand (curb) lane. Ahead of me in the same left hand lane I was in, there were two vehicles; a car, and an SUV. As all four vehicles progressed south on the road, the school bus made stops at the corners of two successive intersections.

With each stop the school bus made, the other three vehicles stopped, as required by state law, until the kids were safely off the bus and the driver had turned off the flashing red lights. There were no stop signs at any of the intersections. In the course of making the two stops, one of the vehicles ahead of me passed the school bus when it resumed progress after the first stop. The distance between the remaining vehicle ahead and my own had closed to the point that we were separated by only a car length or so.

When the school bus resumed travel after the second stop, there was a longer distance ahead before the next stop than the distance between the previous two stops. As the car ahead of me passed the school bus, the bus driver activated the flashing amber lights. At that point in time, my vehicle was alongside the school bus. The school bus continued, slowing very gradually. It appeared to me that the bus driver was being kind enough to allow me to pass before stopping her bus.

As I came abreast of the bus driver's side window, I glanced to my right, intending to give the driver a wave of thanks for letting me go by. At just that moment, the driver slammed the lever deploying the swing out stop sign. Startled by her sudden action, I saw her flash me a dirty look. At that point, my vehicle was already past the front end of the bus and the bus was still slowing for a stop. I glanced into my rear view mirror to get a look at the bus driver, wondering what her problem was. At the same time I noticed a constable's cruiser turning onto the boulevard in the curb lane, far behind us.

The officer was 2,376 feet (.45 miles) behind the school bus. While I noticed the distinctive White, red and blue cruiser turning onto the boulevard as I glanced in my rear view mirror, I didn't give it a second thought. I also observed the driver open the school bus doors and the first child step off the bus.

Approximately 3,000 feet further down the road, I noticed the Constable's cruiser coming up behind me at a rapid clip, red and blue lights flashing. The officer bumped his siren for a moment, as I braked to a stop 3,168 feet (.6 mile) past the point where I had passed the school bus.

I rolled down both my front windows as the officer came up on the passenger side of my vehicle. He asked for my license and proof of insurance. I said to the officer, "Do you mean to tell me that bus driver said I passed her bus while it was stopped?". "No", the officer replied, "she didn't tell me, I saw you myself". Of course, I felt like telling him he was a bald faced liar. But what I did was to make my second mistake. I said something like,"No way! Even if I had passed the bus while it was stopped, which I did not, there is no way you could have seen it from as far away as you were."

It must have been an off day for my brain. Actually it was more likely the result of being out of practice, since I had not had a ticket in more than five years. My first mistake was to ask the question about the driver telling the officer I had passed her stopped school bus.

Asking the first question and making the comment about the distance factor was very foolish. I should not have said a word, except to answer any direct question he might have asked. For example, if he had asked if I realized I passed a school bus that was stopped and discharging passengers, I should have answered that question, simply saying, "No, I did not do that."

After the officer handed me the citation, I put it into my wallet, started my car, drove to the next crossover and made a U-turn. I drove back to the Avenue from which the officer had turned onto the boulevard. I followed the road to the critical points and recorded the distances. Next, I retrieved my Polaroid camera from my office and took several photographs. Then I wrote out my notes of all I could recall of the entire incident.

In reviewing my options, I decided that I would take traffic school instead of fighting the ticket. The reason is simple . . . to save money that I couldn't save if I went to court and **won** the case.

Here's how it works. My insurance company, at that time, gave a fifteen percent discount off my insurance premium for taking a defensive driving course. What's more, the discount remained in effect over a period of three years. At $860. Per year for my insurance, a fifteen percent discount comes to $129. per year. Over a three year period, that is a saving of $387.00. The cost of attending the defensive driving course, including the fees for the court, would total about $100.00. That would mean three year total savings to me of $278.00. That's my idea of a pretty good deal. These days, many Insurance companies no longer give discounts for defensive driving courses. And the ones that still do, offer more like ten percent discounts. Add to the increased court fees and course fees and it is not nearly as attractive as it once was.

But, imagine my surprise, when I went to the courthouse on October 20, 1997 and informed the clerk that I had decided to take traffic school on the ticket instead of paying the fine or going to trial. (Another good thing about the traffic school option is that upon completion of the course, the ticket gets dismissed and does not go into my driving record as a conviction.)

I was astonished, when the clerk informed me that Judge So and So (in whose court I was required to appear) "does not allow traffic school on school bus tickets." I was further informed that the Judge "is tough on school bus tickets, and levies a $1,000.00 fine." (The judge, paragon of virtue that he was, by the way, was later thrown out of office for sexual harassment charges by some of his women staff).

I was left with two options (unless, of course, I chose to walk into court, plead guilty, hand my checkbook to the judge, and ask him to please write out a check for any amount his heart desired). I could request a court trial, that is, a trial before a judge . . . in this case a judge who refuses to allow traffic school and levies a thousand dollar fine. Or, alternatively, I could request (Demand) a trial before a jury. I have never had a masochistic streak in my personality. Thus it came to pass that on October 20, 1997, I submitted to the court my written request for a jury trial. My written request included a directive that I wanted the school bus driver subpoenaed to appear at the trial to give sworn testimony.

Nothing happened. Days passed, filling out calendar pages of weeks, then months. The passage of months filled a full year. Still the days wore on. In the first week of January, 1999, as I performed my annual ritual of going through my files and culling outdated material, I came across the file I had put together in September 1997, on the evening of the day I received the citation, sixteen months earlier. **Sixteen months!** So much for the concept of one's constitutional right to a speedy trial of one's peers. At this rate, my peers would all be dead of old age before my trial. Okay, I figured, the thing must have been dismissed and they forgot to notify me. That was okay, I thought.

The most astonishing part was yet to come. In late May 1999, I received in the mail a Notice of Jury Trial, set for June 10, 1999. Immediately I began calling the clerk's office. I called at least a dozen times over a period of two or three days, with no success. I drove to the courthouse and went to the clerk's office. When I asked, I was told the school bus driver had not been subpoenaed.

Outraged, I was told by the clerk that the officer was being sent to get the name of the driver. If he could get her name and address, I was told, the court would send her a letter, requesting her to appear at the trial, but would not issue a subpoena. Boy! Wouldn't that be grounds for reversal on appeal!

I was angry over the pathetic condition of the court. Judge Romeo (not his real name) had not yet been kicked out and was still busy chasing after the ladies. The people who intended to snatch a thousand dollars of my hard earned money; take bread from my family's table; apparently did not know; or did not care that the Sixth Amendment of the United States Constitution guarantees me and everyone the right to a speedy trial. That same amendment guarantees my right to have compulsory process for obtaining witnesses in my favor. I was beginning to fantasize about the Joy of winning on Appeal.

To help myself prepare for trial, I decided to purchase a copy of the state traffic laws. Oh Boy! I drove to the closest office of the Texas Department of Transportation and was told that in our state, you must purchase the traffic laws book from the local Department of Public Safety (Highway patrol) office. So, I walked the half block to the DPS office. I told the receptionist I wanted to buy a copy of the traffic laws handbook. She gave me a world class blank look, then a couple of blinks and replied, "You want to buy a copy of the traffic laws . . .?"

The lady made two or three phone calls to different people in the office until she succeeded in getting a gentleman to come forward. He looked me up and down, as if he never seen one of these before. Then he told me I was at the wrong department. He said I had to go to the Department of transportation if I wanted to purchase a copy of the traffic laws.

I explained that I had just come from the DOT office and that they told me the DPS office was where I had to go to buy the handbook. The DOT lady had been kind enough to let me look through her own copy of the handbook. Sure enough, right there in the handbook itself, it said in plain English that copies of the manual or handbook could be purchased at the local office of the DPS.

Next, I was told to have a seat until sergeant so and so could see me.. I waited and in about fifteen minutes sergeant so and so stepped up to me and told me to follow him to his office. Once there, he invited me to have a seat.

The sergeant informed me that he had no copies of the handbook to sell me. He made a call to his state headquarters and got someone there to fax an order form, which he gave me, telling me I could order the handbook by *mail*. I did not have time to order the book by mail and wait for two weeks or so to receive it.

My next move was to visit the public library. I would review the handbook and copy whatever pages or passages I would need to prepare my case. The Library did not have a copy of the handbook. The reference Librarian and I searched unsuccessfully for it. Though the catalogue said it was there, we could not find it. The lady said she would search further and call me if she found it.

Calls to several bookstores in the area provided me with the information the distribution of the handbook had been pulled from the company that had handled it for years. The book was no longer available to commercial book stores. By that time, I was losing what little patience I had left.

The next thing I did was call my Local State Representative (who has gone on to the U. S. Congress, not in my District). I expressed my complaint about the restrictive access the public had to *buying* the handbook. I said this is a book that should be readily available to any and every resident of the state who wants to buy a copy of it *today*. I'm sorry to report that my State Rep was no help at all.

Time was drawing near for my trial and I was hampered in my preparations by the lack of access to the handbook. Then I received a call from the Librarian, telling me she had found the handbook, misfiled in the wrong place. I drove over to the Library, studied the handbook, made copies of a few relevant sections, thanked the lady and went home to complete my trial preparations.

At that point, I was raring to go to trial, looking forward to it! I was loaded with Constitutional citations and several dismissal motions based upon them. If the judge turned out to be the one who did not subscribe to the rights guaranteed to Americans by the United States Constitution, I was supremely confident that he would get a valuable lesson from the appeals court down the line.

But life, as we all know, is full of surprises . . .

On the day of my trial, I stopped into the clerk's office before going into the courtroom to see if the school bus driver had been subpoenaed. I learned that she had not been subpoenaed, went into the courtroom and took a seat.

The docket was called. After my name was called and I answered, I started a conversation with another gentleman, who was also there for trial. My citation was *twenty-one* months old as we sat in court that day. I was astounded to learn that the other gentleman's citation was *thirty-three* months old!

After waiting another forty minutes, the prosecutor called out the names of thirteen of us who were there for trial, announced that our cases had been dismissed and we were free to go. It turned out that those thirteen cases ranged from eighteen months old to more than three years old. *Incredible*, I thought! I have since learned that pretty much the same scenario was played out twice a month in that particular judge's court, which is no longer his court. I think such a lack of performance is worse than incredible. In my opinion, that is criminal.

But, there it was, another day, in another traffic court, and another Victory . . . however empty it seemed at the time.

The final anecdote I will relate to you, occupies the opposite end of the spectrum of the story you just read. It was remarkable in its simplicity, distinguished by the good will and good sense that was applied to the situation.

Here is what happened. My Wife's Mother had been very ill for several years and passed away in the nursing home, where she had lived for the last year of her life when she left us to go to Heaven. After her death, her mortal remains were transported to her hometown for her funeral service. A few days after her funeral, I had to go out of town o a business trip. On the Sunday morning after her mother's funeral and with me out of town, my Wife was driving alone to Mass. She was a little pre-occupied with the thoughts of her Mom and the fact that she would not be going to the nursing home to visit her Mother after Mass, as we had done each Sunday for more than a year.

As my Wife turned onto the two lane country road heading for Church, somewhat lost in her thoughts about her Mother, a police car turned onto the same road from the opposite direction, about a mile ahead. The police car had turned onto the road my Wife was on from the road she would be turning onto a mile ahead.

The police car approached and passed her, then made a u-turn, flipped on his flashing lights and signaled my Wife to pull over.

The officer was all business. He asked my Wife if she realized how fast she was driving. She replied that she really didn't know what her actual speed was, but didn't think she was speeding. She told the officer about her Mother's recent death and what she had been thinking about. This was the first Sunday in a long time that she would not be going from Church to the nursing home to visit her Mom.

The officer wasn't paying any attention to what she was saying to him, interrupting her to say that he had clocked her with his radar doing sixty-eight miles per hour in the forty-five mile per hour zone on that country road. He wrote out a citation, handed it to her and told her to drive carefully . . . and have a nice day.

My wife went on to Church and then back home. When I returned from my trip, she told me about the ticket and I looked it over. I asked my Wife if the officer had shown her the radar gun or invited her to take a look at it if she wished. He had not. I said I believed she could go to court on the tickedt and win, but traffic school would be a better option. The savings on her car insurance from the defensive driving discount would cancel out the cost of the course and leave a couple of hundred dollars in savings over the next three years.

A few days before her scheduled court appearance date, my Wife and I went to the municipal court clerk's office in the small town where she received the ticket. I was getting the school option set up with the clerk for my Wife. I told the clerk I didn't know who the officer was that gave my Wife the ticket, but that he was a "rat", whoever he was. The lady asked me why and I related the details of how my Wife came to get the ticket.

The clerk told me I should go talk to the Chief of Police. I said something like, "Oh sure". "No, really", she said. "He's a very nice man. He's in the Building right behind this one. If you want to go talk to him I'll just hold this paperwork here until you've talked to him. Then you can let me know if we should proceed with it". I thought about it for a moment and told her I would just do that.

My Wife and I walked around to the Police Headquarters building, went inside and asked to see the Chief. A few minutes later a Lieutenant came out to the Lobby, told us the Chief was not in and asked if there was anything he could help us with. I explained why we were there and the Lieutenant said we should talk to the Captain in charge of the Patrol Division, but that the Captain was at lunch.
I told the Lieutenant my Wife and I would just go have some lunch and come back.

After lunch, we went back to Police Headquarters and met with the Patrol Division Captain. He greeted us and ushered us into his office. The lieutenant had filled him in on the reason we were there. We chatted for a few minutes and I said, "Well, the long and short of this, I guess, is we're here to ask you to dismiss the ticket."

I told the Captain I wasn't necessarily saying my Wife was not speeding; that I could conceive of the prospect that she, being a little depressed, sad and preoccupied at the time, may indeed have put a little too much foot into her driving. But the sixty-eight miles per hour was not, in my opinion, in the realm of possibility. I know my Wife better than anyone. She wouldn't be driving that fast. Besides, it would have been almost impossible to reach that great a speed in the space of less than half a mile, unless she was fiercely determined to do so. There was also the fact, I reminded the Captain that the officer neither showed nor offered to show the radar gun to my Wife.

The Captain asked my Wife a few questions about how fast she had been driving and the like. She gave all the wrong answers, basically admitting she had no idea what her actual speed was. The Captain was smart and courteous. He saw the situation for what it was. Probably my Wife had been speeding. There was a good chance the speed indicated on the citation was overstated in error. Perhaps it was fifty-eight miles per hour. He also recognized some other factors: my Wife had just buried her Mother and was sad and distracted by that. A jury, if she chose to go to trial would be sympathetic and a strong case could be made that there was no way she could have attained such speed in the distance covered.

The Captain got up from his chair and told us he had no problem with dismissing the ticket under the circumstances. "Just leave the ticket here with me. I'll take care of it", he said. We thanked the Captain for his kind consideration, shook hands and went home, happy.

Now why did the Captain agree to dismiss the ticket? Was it because there was such overwhelming evidence in my Wife's favor that there was no chance the city prosecutor could have won the case in a jury trial? The truth is, I believe the Captain was simply using good sense and showing some old fashioned compassion to another human being.

From the moment the lady in the clerk's office suggested I should speak to the Chief, I sensed that an old fashioned common sense, good neighbor philosophy prevailed in that small town administration. Simple kindness is something you don't see a lot of these days. But I think that's what we found working for us that day.

This much is certain. There are all sorts of ways to win in traffic court. And, as this serves to illustrate, sometimes you can win even before you go to traffic court. But you don't win . . . can't win . . . if you don't try to win. How simple a concept, to be overlooked by so many.

ABOUT DRIVING UNDER THE INFLUENCE

I have never been cited for driving under the influence of drugs or alcohol. I have never used drugs. I do use alcohol. I frequently have wine with dinner and enjoy a cocktail, a beer, an aperitif or glass of wine in social situations and in moderation. I drink responsibly, as anyone who indulges should. The truth is, there were occasions in my younger days when I drove impaired.
Fortunately, I never caused an accident, injury or death as a result. I have matured and disciplined myself.

Too many people die on our highways as a result of drunk or drugged drivers. Don't drink and drive. Don't drive drunk. Don't drive under the influence of drugs. Above all, don't do drugs. Don't become a criminal. Don't become a murderer.

CHAPTER FOURTEEN

Smile, You're On . . .
Crooked Camera

New Ways To Steal Your Money

In the eternal quest to find means of taking more and more money from you, and please understand here that getting your money from you by any way possible is all the Bureaucrats at any level of government exist for . . . these masters of deceit have created a new "mother Lode" for grabbing tens, or what may become hundreds of millions of dollars from hard working, and hard pressed American Families.

By now, surely everyone in America is aware of the "Red Light Camera" scams. I have researched the Red Light Camera phenomenon and it is clear that cities and towns all across the land have latched onto this scheme. This Machiavellian racket is beyond redemption. Red Light Cameras are a dirty money grab that the perpetrators have attempted to disguise as a safety measure that will reduce accidents and traffic deaths and injuries.

I chose the word *Machiavellian* to describe the Red Light Camera Scheme. I chose the word carefully because it so perfectly fits. The word is used to describe activity that is typically characterized as being marked by cunning, duplicity, or bad faith. To gain even more perspective, let's look at some **Synonyms** for the word Machiavellian, such as, Cutthroat, Immoral, Unprincipled, Unconscionable, Unethical and Unscrupulous. Then we could also look at a few **Antonyms** for the word, like, Ethical, Moral, Principled and Scrupulous. It is interesting that I have seen the Synonyms listed above mentioned in numerous challenges and lawsuits against jurisdictions that have installed (and in numerous cases have had to remove) the cameras. Never have I seen any of those Antonyms (opposites) to the word Machiavellian used to describe the merits of the scheme, nor do I ever expect to.

To keep the record straight here, I will state, clearly and without hesitation or reservation, that I am 100 % opposed to: The Red Light Camera Scam. I consider it nothing more than a thinly veiled attempt to steal money from the public. That said, I will add that I am not writing here to influence your own evaluation or opinion of the subject Cameras and their use.

What I will offer in this chapter is anecdotal information concerning my own experience with the process, the circumstances of the citations (I was cited on two separate occasions at different locations), the conditions and details of the locations, my responses and the outcomes. Then, I invite you to judge for yourself whether or not the Red Light Cameras are, as I stated above, *a thinly veiled attempt to steal money from the public.*

In this chapter you will learn all of the details of the two Red Light Camera tickets I have personally received, the first one at 12:13 P.M., November 22, 2009, and the second at 6:48 P.M., August 7, 2010. I will identify them as SCAM No. 1 and SCAM No. 2. I will relate all of the circumstances and reveal the strategies I applied to achieve victory.

SCAM NO. 1

On or about November 26, 2009 I received a letter from the Photo Red light Enforcement Program office of the City that cited me (which shall remain nameless, as I do not wish to bring shame or embarrassment upon the citizens of the place, some of whom are good friends of mine) informing me that I was cited by a Red Light Camera for running a red light at a major intersection at 12:13 p.m. November 22, 2009. Included was a photo showing my wife's car crossing the intersection limit line. The speed limit on the street was 30 mph. The speed limit on the cross street (a State Highway) was 45 mph.

My first reaction was to wonder when my wife got the citation. When I checked the date on the ticket and looked at the calendar it immediately became clear that the day was a Sunday. The time revealed that it was after the 10:30 a.m. Mass we always attend, which also meant that I was the driver at the time. *I do not run red lights.* I also do not stop in intersections . . . unless there is a sudden blockage

Also included in the letter was a website address where, I was informed, I could go to view the video of the alleged violation. I was steamed, especially when I noted the fact from the enclosed photos that the left side of my front bumper had clearly already crossed the limit line. That meant that my car was in the intersection and stopping in an intersection is itself, a violation. [A short aside here: the two streets at the intersection where I was cited are not exactly perpendicular. Thus the limit line and crosswalks on the street I was driving on are angled approximately thirty degrees from one side to the other.] At that point, there was one thing I knew for certain: I had a lock on Victory.

I went to the hearing and challenged the citation. The hearing officer . . . a seriously obese police officer in plain clothes and a man of few words played the video and glanced at the photos. He announced his "Finding" that I was "Liable". He then informed me that I would have to post a $50.00 fee to have a "Trial Di Novo" set for a future date. I posted the fee on that day, 1/12/2009, and went home to await the notice for the "Trial Di Novo", before a Municipal Judge.

Because the end result of the **SCAM NO. 1** case did not occur until long after the **SCAM NO. 2** Red light Camera Citation, I will relate to you all of the details of that second Scam, before finishing the story of the first . . .

SCAM NO. 2

I received the second citation in another jurisdiction nearby on 8/7/2010 at 6:48 p.m. The event occurred at an intersection of a Freeway Feeder Road. I was driving in the westbound curb lane, preparing to make a right turn. This intersection has two right turn lanes into a three northbound lane street. Opposing southbound traffic on that street is also three lanes, separated by a wide, landscaped esplanade. The right turn arrow is normally green, except when the crossing northbound traffic light turns green. At that point, the right turn arrow on the service road turns red. A right turn on red is permissible, as with any right on red. You must first come to a complete stop.

The right turn arrow was turning red as I approached and I stopped. There was an 18 wheeler in the next lane (also a right turn lane). The 18 wheeler driver, seeing that there was no approaching cross traffic from the left, just cruised into his right turn. Then, I started my right turn . . . a completely legal right on red. Perhaps it was the big rig that triggered the Camera. I can't say for certain. But I had clearly mad a legal right on red.

I went for my hearing at the appointed time. The hearing officer, this time around, not only presented a better and more professional appearance, but was more professional in his actions. He asked if I was challenging the citation and I said, simply, "yes". He ran the video and noted that "We have a big rig here, in the second right turn lane." I said, "Yes and as you can see, my vehicle is stopped in the right lane, prior to

118

starting my turn ". He agreed and said, "okay, I will issue a Not Liable for this and you're good to go." Just like that . . . another victory . . . but a hollow one. Considering the fact that I had to take two hours out of my day and make a twenty five mile round trip, it didn't feel much like a win. However, it was better than handing over seventy-five of my hard earned dollars.

Now, before going on to the rest of the story of SCAM NO.1, Let's take a closer look at this evil Red Light Camera racket, and why I believe such programs should be universally banned in every jurisdiction in America. My personal research has revealed that there are Red Light Cameras in twenty-six States and the District of Columbia throughout the Nation.

The perpetrators of this fraudulent scam would have you believe that they are committed to improving safety at intersections and saving lives. I believe that is a lie. There are numerous studies and surveys that purport to show that the red light cameras have reduced accidents at intersections, or reduced injuries or fatalities. Such claims are overshadowed by studies that reveal mo such reductions and, in many instances and locations actually show increases in injuries and fatalities.

There was a once widespread trait in America that was called "common sense". In our present times, "Common Sense" has become very "Uncommon". The Red light Camera scam has one goal and one goal only . . . to generate massive sums of money for the jurisdictions that use them. That's it! Please do not believe the hogwash about safety. The simple fact is that in many, if not all, of the jurisdictions using these money machine cameras, they have increased the likelihood of crashes and injuries or deaths at the intersections where they are deployed.

Consider this: in many, or most of the red light camera locations, the timing of amber light durations has been reduced. Reducing the duration of the amber light at an intersection by two or three seconds increases the likelihood that more red light camera citations will be issued, bringing more and more dollars into the coffers of that jurisdiction.

The other side of that equation is that by reducing the time of the amber light, the drivers are subjected to the dangerous situation that they do not have enough time to safely stop for the red light and are exposed to increased danger of collision, injury and death.

Remember that when you approach an intersection with a traffic light, when the light turns amber, warning you to stop, there is a period of time required to: First. React to the changing light and then, Second. Safely stop.

My personal contention, based upon my own driving experiences and observations and personal research that I have conducted, is simple and direct. Stopping for a red traffic light comes down to the basic, simple issue of safely bringing the vehicle to a complete stop prior to crossing into the intersection. But, don't confuse the term *basic, simple* with *easy*! The rule is basic and simple . . . light turns red – stop vehicle. However, it is **not** always easy to execute the maneuver. In fact, it is frequently quite difficult to do so.

There are *essential variables* that influence that task, such as the following, for example (not a complete list):
- Posted speed limit for street you are driving on.
- Posted speed limit for the cross street you are approaching;
- The 85 percentile speed on both streets.
- Your actual speed when you first observe the changing light.

- The distance, at your first observation, between the front bumper of your vehicle and the intersection limit line.
- The distance between your rear bumper and the trailing (following) traffic (Car or cars).
- The actual speed of the trailing traffic.
- Condition of the road surface, dry, smooth, rough, wet, icy, snow, rising, descending.
- Visibility (blinding sun or headlights ahead or behind, rain or snow, darkness).
- Number and type of passengers in your vehicle (adults, children, elderly, infants, etc) and where seated.
- Your own health (physical handicap, sleepy or physically tired, mentally distracted by personal issue or issues).

I am certain that you could add other essential variables to this list. The intent here is not to get you to rack you brain for all of the possible variables that could exist or to try to brainstorm a preconceived solution for any and every situation that you could possibly encounter. That would be wasted energy and you would likely forget the solutions you worked out. What's more, even if you constructed a written list of all of those solutions, *you would not have the time to get the list out of the glove box and pick the right solution in time.*

But, relax, all that's not necessary. There are studies that have been conducted to make your task easier and safer. One such study that was conducted by the Institute of Transportation Engineers (ITE) resulted in the calculation of recommended minimum yellow light times for various speed limits:

- 25 MPH - 3.0 seconds
- 30 MPH - 3.5 seconds
- 35 MPH - 4.0 seconds
- 40 MPH - 4.5 seconds
- 45 MPH - 5.0 seconds

- 50 MPH - 5.5 seconds
- 55 MPH - 6.0 seconds

Keep in mind that, these are **Minimum** recommended yellow light durations and the 3.0 second duration is the absolute minimum recommended time for any intersection.

For those of you who like to get into the Math, I recommend that you go to the Web Site of the National Motorists Association (www.motorists.org) and search for the "Yellow Light Time Standards". There you will find a commonly used equation for calculating the duration of the yellow interval that is proposed by the ITE Technical Committee.

Allow me to say more about the National Motorists Association. This is an organization I recommend to all motorists, no matter where you live. The wealth of informative and helpful information to be found on their Web Site is reliable and informative for all motorists. There you will also find many links to information from many sources that are valuable to anyone who drives a vehicle. There are options for membership, including a free option and a great deal more that will help you to be a better and more informed driver. Check it out. I'm sure you will agree.

I will conclude this section by completing my personal contention concerning the red light camera issue. I am completely and unalterably opposed to the cameras because I believe them to be nothing more than a dirty racket employed by the jurisdictions that use them as a means of doing only one thing; accomplishing one goal . . . stealing your money under false pretenses and bolstering that goal by the use of deceit, lies and threats, along with false claims of improved safety.

Now, let's move on to the conclusion of **Scam NO. 1.**

Having posted my $50.00 "Appellate Filing Fee on January 12, 2010, I returned home to await the notification for my "Trial de Novo". I had essentially done all of my research and planning for the trial, but I looked over the paperwork a few times over the following couple of weeks to make sure I was comfortable with everything. I had all of my ducks in a perfect row and was looking forward to a "good time" in court.

What I did not know on January 12, 2010 and the Weeks that followed . . . and the Months that followed . . . and the Years that followed . . . was that I was in for a long wait . . . a REALLY LONG wait.

On April 5, 2012, The City Municipal Court mailed me a notice to "personally appear before the (City Name Deleted) Municipal Court . . . for the purpose of a Trial de Novo in the above referenced matter (Automated Traffic Signal Enforcement Violation No. [# deleted] on: 25th day of April, 2012 at 9:00 AM."

If there was not such a thing in this world as LAUGHTER, I would have been unable to have a response to what I was reading. I cracked up in laughter! What made it all the funnier for me was the fact that only a couple of days earlier, I had seen the old file . . . still on my desktop . . . and had decided that it was probably time for me to file a complaint with the District Attorney's Office.

Needless to say, my trial prep would now have to be modified. I was no longer interested in Limit Lines or yellow light times or photos, or any of that. This was no longer going to be me on trial. In fact, this was no longer going to be a trial at all! I must confess I was giddy about the whole thing . . . couldn't wait for the 25th to arrive! This was not going to be a trial at all. This was going to be an old fashioned butt-kicking and I was going to enjoy every minute of being the one doing the kicking.

I arrived at the court on April 25th at 8:45 a.m., fifteen minutes before the 9:00 a.m. time on the notice to appear. There were two others there when I arrived. The Courtroom was locked, so we waited in the lobby area. Time passed and others arrived. No one bothered to make an announcement of any kind to the seven people who were waiting. At 9:55 a.m., the door was unlocked and a plain clothes police officer informed us in a loud and officious tone that we may . . . "enter the courtroom and take seats, do not take seats in the first row and maintain quiet in the courtroom." A few moments later another plain clothes officer entered the courtroom and declared, "All rise. The (city name deleted) Municipal Court is in session; the Honorable Judge (name deleted) presiding."

Everyone in the courtroom turned to see the judge, a small woman of approximately five feet shuffle through the door and begin to make her way to the bench. I use the term "shuffle" not out of disrespect but, because the lady was garbed in a black judge's robe that was at least twelve inches too long and required that she use both hands to hike up the robe enough to be able to walk in it. The whole scene was a bit comedic. The exchanged glances and grins throughout the courtroom said volumes without a word being spoken.

The judge, a nice, friendly lady; bid good morning to all and began to call the docket. My name was first. I answered present and the judge informed me I could step into a side room across the hall that was visible through an open side courtroom door, and "visit with" the prosecutor.

I was having a hard time keeping a straight face, as the young man across the table composed himself, even to the point of adjusting his facial expression to what I expect he felt was more "official looking" or some such nonsense. He made his best effort at browsing attentively through the paperwork, concluding his study with a brief nod of his head. I feared if this continued on for much longer, I would lose it, and burst out laughing.

Mercifully, he cleared his throat and announced, "Well, I see here that you were cited for this red light violation on November 22, 2009." He paused and thought for a moment. "I am not inclined to pursue this matter and I am going to dismiss this case", he said, almost triumphantly. I looked him in the eye and said, simply, without trying to suppress my grin, "Well that's good, since the Statute is only two years". The change in his facial expression clearly told me he no longer thought of us as friends. Pity! He filled out the dismissal form, signed it, handed it to me and, without looking up said, "you can take this up to the clerk. I thanked him, said, "Have a nice day", and took the form to the clerk/cashier. She took the form, made some entries and handed it back. "You may go", she said. "The case is dismissed'. I waited a moment and said, "okay, now I need the refund of my fifty dollar appeal fee. She informed me I would get a check in the mail no later than May 4, 2012. The Lobby was full of people and I couldn't resist a parting shot. "Well, I hope that's true, I said, because it took you folks two years and fifty three days to send me my notice for the trial de novo." I left to the sound of some assorted chuckles.

The check did not arrive by May 4. I told my wife that Friday that if it didn't arrive on Saturday, I'd be at the District Attorney's Office on Monday to file a complaint. The check arrived on Saturday, May 5. With that, Scam No. 1 came to an unceremonious close.

One side note: The Red Light Camera Battle is not over, but the greed merchants are losing. In the end, the Crooked Camera Racket will be gone.

CHAPTER FIFTEEN

The Birth Of A New Cottage Industry

A Stimulus Package for starving lawyers who can't run fast enough to chase Ambulances

These are perilous times in which we live today. The misery index is someplace in the stratosphere and rising. I wrote that statement and almost immediately realized that the notion of the "misery index" *rising* is absurd. After thinking about it for a while I concluded that, as the misery index is rising . . . our quality of life is *descending*. I would go so far as to say **precipitously descending**.

To counter that, I further concluded that we need more humor in our daily lives to lighten the burdens that are driving that misery index to highs and our quality of life to new lows. My ensuing search for more humor immediately turned up a joke: "What do you call 500 lawyers at the bottom of the sea?" Answer: "A good start." . . . . Ohh, you already heard it . . . Yeah, I know, everybody has heard that one.

But I was on a roll of sorts. You see, these thoughts came to my mind as I was working on the outline for the Revised Edition of this book. I had settled on the subject for the final chapter of the book . . . "Saying Goodbye To Traffic Courts" and knew for certain that I wanted that to be the subject of the final chapter. But here I was, struggling with the idea of what should be the subject of Chapter fifteen.

I kept thinking it had to be something that related to lawyers. Hence the lawyer joke above came to mind. Then I thought, it's true enough that almost everyone likes "Lawyer Jokes" . . . even some lawyers.

But as I reflected further, my thought process took a turn into a different direction. "Wait a minute", I thought out loud, "sure, everybody likes lawyer jokes because, as we all know full well, everybody *hates* lawyers . . . ***until they need one, of course***." And, truth be told, the hate part is hate with a small h.

Let me be clear, also, about my personal position on Lawyers in general. I have known many lawyers and even worked for a few lawyers over the years. Like any other group of people, there are good lawyers and bad ones . . . and a whole lot of "in between" ones. I like, respect, even admire "good" lawyers. I despise the "Bad" ones. I could offer some names here, but that would get me in trouble and I'd need a "good" lawyer to defend me. As far as the prominent ones, you already know who are the good ones and the bad ones . . . so do they!

With lawyers, it seems always to be a love/hate relationship with most people . . . can't live with them/can't live without them. I attribute that to the fact that in most situations where a lawyer or lawyers are involved, it is because either there is something in dispute between parties, or parties are preparing or creating something they do not wish to be disputing over in the future.

I can say, unequivocally, I have no need for a lawyer in traffic court and, from what I have observed, most of the Traffic Court lawyers I have seen in action would find themselves in the lower half of the "in betweeners". I'm just sayin' . . .

After puzzling over it for quite a while, something hit me out of the blue, and I had the subject for Chapter fifteen . . . "The Birth Of a New Cottage Industry".

You see, one of the major contributing factors related to Traffic Court, as everyone knows, is that hundreds of millions of traffic tickets are issued annually all over the country, in every part of it; big cities, suburban bedroom communities, small rural municipalities and towns, you name it! Believe me, this traffic ticket thing *really is Big Business.*

When you start to analyze the larger picture, *other factors* come into view. One of those factors is that there are already so many lawyers cluttering up the landscape . . . and let's be honest here, most of them are shut well out of the big dollar cases, barely able to tread water without some major life support: traffic court equals life support for many of these poor souls.

Well, I have also noted in recent times; say the past two or three years, a growing number of "Speed Traps" all around my little world. I don't get many tickets any more, partly because I don't drive nearly as many miles as I used to drive, partly because I am a better driver than I once was (you know . . . back in the day), and partly because I am more focused on the bigger picture. That said, I am going to relate details of two occasions when I was 'trapped' in two different versions of these speed traps and the "Cottage Industry" they have given rise to.

It used to be that when you were pulled over for a real or a contrived traffic violation, the officer, after reciting his preamble and making his best effort to get you to say something that would almost ensure that you would reap a gloriously guilty verdict in traffic court for your naïve statement or question, would take out his Ticket Book and write you an invitation to appear on some future date at such and such court to answer the charges he cited in his written invitation.

The officer would typically have you sign your promise to appear, hand you your copy of the ticket (at no charge, by the way), invite you to "have a nice day" and drive carefully. He would then mosey back to his cruiser and leave you to read your free ticket to traffic court, while he went off in search of another highway marauder. Nothing else would follow that little tableau (unless, perhaps, you replied with a string of your best curses and epithets) until you appeared on the designated date and time at the court.

I feel reasonably sure that the process as described above continues, unchanged, today in many areas of the nation. That is no longer the case in the area where I live. In our present enlightened age of advanced technology, most of the cops, sheriffs and constables in these parts drive cruisers that are fully outfitted with their own computers, photographic equipment, printers and who knows what other gadgets. So the routine today is different . . . except for the officer's preamble (which, I suspect, may also be recorded these days, the better to catch you with).

These days around here, the officer will collect whatever documents he wants you to produce; license, registration, proof of insurance, etc., take them with him back to his cruiser (where he can sit inside in air conditioned comfort and not have to swelter in the heat. There he will "run you through the computer" to verify that your documentation is legitimate and determine whether or not there are any outstanding warrants for your arrest. An interesting side note that has been developing is that many officers no longer ask for your proof of insurance because, apparently they can get that off their computer as well. You may be likely to hear an officer (if he didn't ask for your proof of insurance and you offer it to him) snarl at you, in a tone of voice that suggests you must be an ignoramus, "I don't need that!"

Now, once you've been "processed . . . computerized, you might say", the officer returns with two 8.5" by 11" sheets of paper. He will have you sign one and return it to him and he'll leave the other one with you (or maybe not[1]) and depart with the usual comments. Then the pageant begins.

Within a few days to a week after the officer hands you your copy of the invitation to appear in Traffic Court, you will begin to see your mail box filling up with "fan Mail" . . . from LAWYERS. All of your new friends will be falling over each other to tell you not to worry about the ticket the mean old officer gave you. They will tell you that they will rescue you for a fee starting at a mere $25.00 . . . No worries, Mate! Each day, right up to the time of your court date you will find more of these life-saving letters in your mailbox. This is the stimulus package mentioned in the sub-title of this chapter. Think of it as Welfare for Starving Lawyers.

Let's take a look now, at my first "Trapped" episode. I call it the ***"Deputy Dirty Dawg Caper No.1"***. Here's what happened:

At about 11:00 a.m. on a clear morning, I am driving a company car along in the number one, right hand lane of a Country Farm road with the cruise control set at the 55 MPH speed limit. The highway has two lanes in each direction separated by a center left turn either way lane. There is virtually no other traffic visible to me in either direction, until I notice a Sheriff Deputy's cruiser coming into view from the opposite direction at a pretty rapid clip. The cruiser is in the number one lane, next to the left turn lane. The distance between our vehicles closes very quickly as the deputy approaches and then blows by me at a high rate of speed, though his flashing lights were not turned on.

As the cruiser sped past me, I glanced into my rear view, wondering where he was going in such a hurry. Then his brake lights came on and he literally squealed into a slip-sliding U-Turn. I was stunned as I noticed him activate his "party lights" and accelerate in my direction. I muttered something along the lines

130

of: "What the hell is this guy up to?" He moved into my lane and I slowed, turned on my right turn signal, pulled off the highway onto the shoulder, came to a stop and shut down the engine. I rolled down the passenger side window as he walked toward my car.

The deputy was a very stocky, late thirties looking guy with a world class scowl on his face. He bent toward the open side window and shouted . . . yes, SHOUTED . . . "Do you know what the speed limit is here?"

He was speaking (shouting) rapid fire and his eyes were darting in every direction . . . so much so that I glanced in a couple of directions to see what his darting eyes were looking at. "Yes", I said, "The speed limit is 55 and that's what I had my cruise control set on." Then, again in such rapid fire speech that I consciously wondered if he was high on something, he ordered me to produce my driver's license and proof of insurance.

I was driving a company vehicle on company business. I got out my driver's license and then retrieved from the glove box a document we carried that informed that the company was self insured in accordance with the requirements of State law. I explained that to him as I handed over the document. I should mention here that the company is a multi-billion dollar firm that conducts business on every continent.He took the two documents and walked back to his cruiser. He was gone for so long that I wondered aloud, "What the hell is he doing back there?"

A few minutes later, after I'd been waiting almost fifteen minutes, he reappeared at the window. He handed my documents back to me and then passed an 8.5" by 11"sheet of paper to me and kept a second such sheet in his hand. In the same rapid fire delivery accompanied by those darting eyeballs he ordered me to sign the paper and hand it back to him, which I did. Then he really floored me. "I'm not going to give you this other copy, because I'm going to void this citation and I need this copy to get my credit."

With his rapid fire speech, I barely understood his words. Moreover, what he said did not make any sense to me. However, if cop stops me and subsequently says he's going to void the citation, you will not see me give him any argument. I was convinced in my own mind that the guy was either drunk (though I did not detect any scent of alcohol) or stoned. He literally sprinted back to his cruiser, whipped out onto the pavement, made another of his slip sliding U-Turns and sped away. In all of my long life, I never had an experience like this one. It was unique among every traffic stop I have ever had!

In the days that followed, I wondered how this weird event would play out. Would I just receive a notice in the mail that my citation had been voided? This was a new one on me. I had no idea what to expect. I certainly did NOT expect what actually followed.

About a week after my strange traffic stop, I received a letter from a Law Firm, informing me that "Docket records" at a Justice of the Peace court about thirty miles away from the point where the citation was issued "indicate you received the following citation(s): TICKET NUMBER XXXXX, OFFENSE DESCRIPTION SPEEDING, FINE AMOUNT $150.00 Total Fines (estimated) $150.00 The citation was issued on a country road in a small town outside the city limits of the jurisdiction where the Justice of the Peace court cited in the letter from the Law firm was located. I had not received ANY notices from the court cited in the Law Firm letter. Moreover, there was a Justice of the Peace court, about ten miles from the point where the citation was issued, and within the Precinct boundaries of that court.

It made no sense why the ticket would be answerable at the court thirty miles away and inside the boundaries of another jurisdiction.

Obviously, the Deputy Sheriff who withheld my copy of the citation *because he was going to void the citation and needed my copy to **get His Credit***, was a damn liar! I spoke to a friend I worked with who was a retired Sheriff's Deputy about the episode. He asked for the name of the Deputy and I couldn't give to him because I had not received my copy of the citation. My friend told me to go to the JP Court and get a copy of the citation. I did that and then gave the name of the Deputy to my friend. He told me he knew about the guy and that the guy was bad news, a scammer, and worse.

I wracked my brain over how to handle the mess. As I saw things, I had three options. I could file a complaint with the sheriff's Department about the renegade deputy. I could file a complaint with the County District Attorney. Or, I could first address the matter to the court. I reasoned that a complaint to either the Sheriff's Department, which was already defending itself against numerous charges of violations by Deputies, or the District Attorney's office which was defending itself in Grand Jury Investigations and FBI investigations into possible criminal charges against the Department and/or the Sheriff, would be the wrong way to go.

I wrote to the Judge of the Court an explained the entire process I'd been through, gave him all the particulars, and requested that he recognize the situation for what is was and dismiss the case. The actual citation was not in the court. It had been filed electronically and no paper copy had been received by the court.

I stated that I would not sit still for such an outrageous hijacking of Justice and would file complaints and charges with every law enforcement unit in the County if I had to, including the possibility of criminal charges against the renegade deputy, with a hint that I had friends inside the Sherriff's department who would substantiate my charges against the deputy. I concluded my letter by stating that in the event that he would not summarily dismiss the case, then my letter was to serve as my request for a jury trial.

I would bet that you have already come to the conclusion that the judge did not dismiss. Touché. But don't get too big a head . . . the odds were stacked against any summary dismissal . . . if for no other reason, perhaps, than that the judge wanted to see the show in court when this outlaw deputy and I went at it.

Eventually I received a notice to appear for my jury trial. There was a problem, though. Our granddaughter was getting married in another city, two hundred miles away on the day after the trial date. As part of the Wedding Party, my wife and I had obligations to attend two functions the day before the wedding (the trial date). Thus, it was necessary to have the case reset, which was done without any problem. I subsequently received a new notice to appear on a date a couple of months hence.

The next problem reared its head about a week prior to the new trial date, when I received a notice to appear in one of the Civil District Courts in a private matter that had been ongoing for some time. I was definitely not favorably disposed to reset the matter in the District Court, but I didn't have to. Regardless of the fact that the traffic case had already been reset previously, as if to underline the lowly estate of the traffic courts in the judicial pecking order, the district court matter automatically takes precedence and the traffic case had to be reset once again. I filed my notice for the reset and waited for the new date . . . And waited . . . And waited. After another month had passed, I contacted the court and asked what was holding everything up. The clerk I spoke to could not find the case file. She informed me that it appeared that the judge had the file.

Two more weeks passed and I called once again. This time, I learned from the clerk that the case had been dismissed a week earlier. As I had not received any such notification I asked the clerk, as politely as I could, to please email me a copy of the dismissal, which she was happy to do. Go Figure! I won, but have no real idea of how or why. After reflecting on the matter far longer than I wanted to I forced myself to accept the fact that it didn't matter. A win is a win, however you look at it. What I believe in my own mind is that the judge, seeing how these delays kept popping up and having read the detailed protest I sent him, and possibly having done a little investigating of his own . . . which I know would have presented him with some troubling facts about the deputy, probably saw the writing on the wall and decided, who needs this crap?

Deputy Dirty Dawg Caper No. 2

This case was a whole lot simpler and un-convoluted, when compared with the previous case . . . but no less disgusting and disgraceful for the Sheriff's Department.

Driving southbound on a local State Highway through what I will describe as a transitional area I was flagged down by a deputy who was parked on the right side shoulder, well off the road in the weeds. His vehicle was a marked SUV. He had a radar gun in his hand when he flagged me down, though I did not ever see him direct the radar gun toward my car.

The posted speed on the State Highway was 65 MPH to a point approximately 1.5 miles before the point where I was flagged down, where the posted speed changes to 60 MPH. At a point approximately half a mile past the 60MPH sign, the highway begins to rise to cross over another highway. At the point where the highway begins its rise there is a yellow diamond shaped sign (These are informational signs) within the yellow diamond there is a white sign with the number 50 and an upward pointing arrow above the number. Presumably, the purpose of this sign (and probably the reason it was posted by the Department of

Transportation) would be to warn drivers that the speed limit changes once again up ahead, to 50 MPH.

Keep in mind, though, that accomplished "Speed Trappers" seldom miss an opportunity to latch onto an ideal Speed Trap set up. And so it is that the Sheriff's Department in the jurisdiction, as well as one of the local Police Departments set up to operate their "pot of gold" almost as soon as the informational sign was installed. It was a perfect spot for them to ply their crooked trade and jack up the revenue streams of both departments. I'm sure they were thinking, "How good can it get?"

I was driving southbound on the State Highway with my cruise control set at 65. When I approached the 60 MPH sign, I reduced my cruise control to 60 MPH and continued south. I noted the informational sign that warned of the 50 MPH speed limit ahead. I was already familiar with the change. When I had passed over the other highway and was approximately a quarter of a mile away from the 60 MPH sign, Deputy Dirty Dawg flagged me down. I pulled off the road onto the right shoulder and rolled to a stop. I did my best to roll far enough forward to afford Deputy Dirty Dawg an opportunity to walk off some of his fat and rolled down my passenger side widow. He approached and said, "Do you know how fast you were driving?" "Yes". I replied, " I do. I was driving with my cruise control set at the speed limit, which is 60 MPH." He gave me a little smirk and said, "No. the Speed Limit is 55 MPH". In fact, at no point along that stretch of highway is the speed limit 55 MPH. So I simply said, "No, it is not. The speed limit here is 60MPH and changes to 50 MPH about a quarter mile ahead, as you can see, just before the traffic light. He collected my documents, went back to his SUV (Would someone please tell me why Cops need to have expensive SUV's, paid for by the taxpayers, to sit in the weeds next to a highway and pull people over for manufactured traffic violations?). When he returned, he handed me my 8.5"X 11" traffic citation printout. This guy was a real scum bag. He cited me for 71 MPH in a 55

MPH zone. That put me in the speed range that raised the fine amount. Yes, he was a Liar . . . No, he was a Damn Liar!

The next week did not provide me with the collection of letters from Lawyers. I was surprised, especially since the citation was to be answered at the same JP court as the Deputy Dirty Dawg case, both of which were far from the nearest Justice of the Peace Precinct. What flooded my mailbox, instead, was an abundance of letters and postcards from Defensive Driving outfits. Thus, it appears that the "Cottage Industry" exists not just to support lawyers who can't run fast enough to chase ambulances, but also to provide a steady flow of customers for the Defensive Driving "schools".

I really wanted to go to court on this one and shred the pathetic deputy when I got him on the stand. But, common sense grabbed me and I decided, instead, to take the defensive driving option for two reasons. First. I knew I would enjoy the camaraderie in the group. And, Second. After calculating the cost to take defensive driving and factoring in the discount on my insurance I came out ahead. I guess I'm just getting old. But I can tell you this with absolute certainty . . . I will never give up my crusade to stand up for my rights and to turn the tables on the perpetrators of greed that will do anything to steal my hard earned money.

CHAPTER SIXTEEN

Saying Goodbye To Traffic Courts

Getting rid of the Traffic Court Thieves is a "No-Brainer" . . . if you have the guts to fight.

"Oh, I'm just going to go ahead and Pay it". I've heard that phrase from hundreds of people I've known over the many decades of my crusade against the Curse of The Traffic Courts . . . most recently from my own daughter and then, right after she finished relating the circumstances of a ticket she received that there is no way she could be convicted of the trumped up "offense". "I just don't want to waste all the time it takes", she told me. But the simple fact is . . . it does not take all that much time if you do things right. I'm still working on her and hoping I'll convince her to get a jury trial, go to court and kick butt! Knowing the details of the citation, I am 100% CERTAIN she will win. And, more importantly, I know how great she will feel when she wins. When you win once, and set your mind to it, you can win almost always.

So let's take a hypothetical look at a blueprint for, once and for all, ridding ourselves of the phony Traffic Court System that steals such enormous amounts of money from the general American Economy.

As a baseline, let's assume that a mere one million traffic tickets are issued each month, nationwide. Next, let's assume that two percent of the people who received those tickets are very righteous individuals, believe they are guilty as charged and decide they want to pay the ticket. Okay. Now we have 980,000 folks who still have a ticket to Traffic Court. Then, let's take it another GIANT step forward. Let's have ALL of those 980,000 people demand their right to a jury trial . . . or even just a court trial. How long do you think it would take to schedule and complete those trials? How many weeks or months do you think some of those more "productive" ticket writing cops would be in court all day, every day, during that time span?

Let's look even further. How far behind do you suppose the system would fall in the second month . . . the third month, and on and on? Are you getting the picture?

The simple question is: How long would it take to completely overwhelm the entire system, Nationwide, if we all decided, collectively, all of us who ever get a ticket, to demand our "day in court"?

No . . . I can hear you asking if I live in a fantasy world . . . if I actually believe that the powers that be would sit still for such a brazen mutiny. No, I do not live in fantasy land. But if you would deny me the simplicity of my proposed solution to the corruption of the Traffic Court System, then you must also deny yourself the simplicity of what you believe the System could do to stifle the mutiny.

So, where does that leave us? I could spend several hours here constructing possible scenarios that the System could develop to respond to the Mutiny and the scenarios that would be developed in response by the Mutineers. Are you getting the picture yet? If this little *passion play* saw both sides jump into high gear, things could . . . things **would** get very nasty, very quickly. Perhaps the Traffic Court System, as it exists today, would crumble and fall in upon itself. Perhaps not. But either way, the situation would create many crises that would be extremely disruptive and dangerous. What that tells me is that it would require a more finessed approach to bringing down the corrupt Traffic Court System as we see it today. I see the courage of individuals to fight the corruption and demand their right to trial as the means to victory.

Using a phased approach is the key to accomplishing that victory. I do not propose abolishing the Traffic Court System and *not replacing it with a more legitimate, more responsible and more effective means of providing traffic safety and promoting better skills and performance by all drivers*. I do believe, though that we can never accomplish the latter condition unless and until we abolish the former. Good things never come easy. It takes hard work and commitment to accomplish worthwhile goals in any part of life.

What I believe is the key is the formation of an association of regional groups of individuals who are committed to cleaning out the corruption of the present system and replacing that corruption with conscientious reforms that will encourage all drivers to be more conscientious and more skillful. Then, using the key of demanding the right to trial and introducing and promoting creation of productive reforms that do not steal the public's hard earned money and, instead, make the roads and highways safer from bad drivers and crooked cops and courts.

I propose to you that the Traffic Court System, Nationwide, in varying degrees, is broken and does virtually nothing to make the roads safer and drivers more conscientious and skillful. Fixing that is a major undertaking, without question. However, I also believe very strongly that "If you can perceive it . . . you can achieve it". If I were a younger man, I would take responsibility to organize a group to start the process.

VOLUNTEERS? . . . MAY I HAVE A SHOW OF HANDS?

AFTERWORD

Some final thoughts . . .

To all who purchase this book; I sincerely thank you. We writers come in all sizes, shapes and persuasions. If there is one common thread that holds us together as an identifiable group, one characteristic common among us, I believe it is surely the notion that we believe we have something of value to offer to others. Whether an author writes to entertain, amuse, educate, influence, inspire, impress, or whatever else I could list here, it is most essential to every writer that his or her work is read.

Most writers, I believe, pursue the craft for numerous reasons, not just one. Perhaps to my detriment, I have never been one to be motivated to do anything strictly for the money. Nor have I been one in search of fame or celebrity status, for in the attainment of those things, the serenity of a private life is lost.

Beyond the desire that their works be read, I believe writers feel a somewhat urgent, underlying wish to be understood. There is a daunting sense of vulnerability . . . and I believe even very seasoned and successful writers are included, that hovers over a writer in the course of creating a work intended to be presented to and read by an audience which may or may not be interested; may or may not accept, approve or enjoy the finished work.

It is my own sincere wish that this book will entertain and enlighten or educate my readers and also serve as an inspiration, to all who read it, to preserve and protect the many rights and freedoms we Americans are so blessed with. I hope that reading the anecdotes presented here will move you to laughter, make you pause and think about your precious rights, the underlying threads of corruption that have produced such decay in the Traffic Court Systems of our Nation, and the impact of that decay in our lives. I especially hope that what you have read here will give you the courage to fight for your precious rights, using the system, and ultimately experiencing the great satisfaction of victory in Traffic Court. Ah, the sweet thrill of Victory!

Writing this book has been fun for me. Living the Traffic Court Adventures I have related to you here though, was a real Hoot. It has always been my way to be a player in life, instead of just being a spectator. Something inside tells me that's the way it is supposed to be. Have you ever noticed the way the winners and losers in any sporting event conduct themselves? It always appears to me that the losers *look* like losers. They seem to be watching the game **happen** to them. The winners, in contrast, are busy **playing** the game, **winning** the game and having a great time.

As a kid, growing up on the streets of Brooklyn, New York, I learned many lessons. One of the early lessons I learned enabled me to compensate for my relatively small size when situations arose, where my friends and I were set upon by a gang of hoodlums on the street while passing through a tough neighborhood. It happened several times. I discovered, practiced and mastered the unknown art of what I call "agricultural warfare". I discovered it accidently, but quickly realized the great value of its equalizing power. I will explain.

At all times, away from my own neighborhood, I carried a few HOT RED PEPPERS in my pockets. When attacked by a hostile bunch of hooligans, I would retreat and assume a defensive sort of crouch, with my hands in my pockets crushing those peppers. Then, as I was being attacked, I would raise my hands as if in defense and immediately rub both my hands in the eyes of the tough guy who thought he was going to beat the heck out of me. SURPRISE! At that point, the toughest of them would start screaming and want no more part of a fight that I didn't want either. I always had all the time I needed for a quick exit.

Now, that story has nothing to do with Traffic Court, of course. But it gives you a little insight into why I am so determined not to be fleeced and bullied by a corrupt bunch of Hooligans in traffic court any more than to be beaten up by a pack of street thugs. I see them as pretty much the same kind of decay.

My experiences in Traffic Court have taught me that, if I prepare myself and conduct myself in a way that shows I take my rights seriously, and believe in the system, it's almost impossible to lose.

So the next time I get a traffic ticket, you know where I will go. I will go to traffic school. If the judge does not allow that option, I will go to court and fight my ticket. I will probably win. I usually do. I believe, if you were to receive a citation and, denied the traffic school option, went to court and struck a blow for freedom, chances are excellent that you would also win.

Good luck. God bless you and, Please, as we say in Texas, Drive Friendly.